IT'S ALL ABOUT

JESUS

THE LIVING WORD

31 DEVOTIONS CONNECTING
EVERYDAY LIFE TO GOD'S WORD

DEBORAH BEDSON

IT'S ALL ABOUT JESUS THE LIVING WORD

GOING DEEPER

This book is meant to be used as a supplement to a regular Bible reading plan.

To dig deeper into God's Word and to make your study richer, it is recommended that you read each passage listed in its full context. That is, read the entire chapter the scripture is pulled from.

FREE RESOURCE

If you would like to have corresponding journal pages, you can download them for no charge at:

https://mailchi.mp/bc40a4e2e162/itsallaboutjesusthelivingword

You will be emailed a PDF file.

Or you can contact us at:

itsallaboutjesusthelivingword@gmail.com

Happy studying, and may God increase your knowledge of His Word.

DEDICATION

To all the readers of this book--whether you are a full-blown Jesus Freak, desiring to grow deeper in your walk with the Lord, or you are seeking to find the love that Jesus so richly wants to give you, it is my prayer that you find peace, hope, strength and joy as you traverse through the pages.

"Let the word of Christ dwell in you richly in all wisdom, teaching and admonishing one another in psalms and hymns and spiritual songs, singing with grace in your hearts to the Lord." (Colossians 3:16)

TABLE OF CONTENTS

INTRODUCTION

To me, there is nothing better than curling up on the couch with a steaming mug of coffee, or on my garden bench with a tall glass of iced tea and my Bible. Digging into God's Word has a profound difference in how my day goes, or more specifically, how I handle things in my day!

The purpose of this devotional is to know Jesus better. It is amazing how intertwined His Word is with our everyday lives. Some people feel they can't understand or relate to the Bible. I hope that by taking time to meditate on the scriptures, you will be able to apply God's truth to your life.

HOW THIS CAME ABOUT

It's All About Jesus-the Living Word came to fruition quite by accident. I was watering my garden one summer day. As I sprayed my sweet peas, I started pondering the different requirements each variety of the plants around me had. Some wanted full sun, while others thrived in the shade. Proper watering ranged from a daily soaking to every few days. Whatever the varying degrees of needs, the bottom line is they all required the same essential elements: Water, soil, and light. These observations led me to compare how different we humans are, yet so much alike. Tall, short, thin, heavy, shy, outgoing; the list goes on. But whatever our traits are, we all have the same basic necessities to survive-food, water, and air.

There is something else we all need, and that is Jesus. We need a Savior. Granted, a lot of people would disagree with that statement. But it doesn't make it untrue. We were created by God Almighty to have a relationship with Jesus. What do we get in exchange? A love so deep and profound it cannot be measured!

So back to my garden pondering. As I continued thinking along these lines, it occurred to me how so much of the Bible relates to our everyday living. God's Word has an answer for every situation we encounter. For example, are you experiencing anxiety? God tells us not to fear; He is with us. Have you lost hope? He tells us He is the Everlasting Hope. Are you dealing with the "S" word? (Sin!) Some passages tell us how to repent, how to avoid it, how we can find forgiveness. Stories and scriptures flashed across my mind, and the next thing I knew this book was coming to life!

~~~~~~~

Each devotional is set up to address a specific topic — hope, fear, sin, prayer, etc. A story is presented, with correlating scriptures and some commentary for your consideration. There are 31 devotions. One can easily be completed in a day. Or, if you want to dig deeper into the passages, take a few days. The pace is entirely up to you.

HOW TO GET THE MOST OUT OF YOUR STUDY TIME:

1. Before you start, pray for God to give you understanding and new insights into His Word.

2. Read through the devotion.

3. Get a notebook and pen and jot down thoughts, impressions, and questions as you read the passages.

4. Go deeper into the study by looking up the scripture, and read the entire chapter it comes from, so you can understand the context.

5. Reflect on what you read, and consider your responses as you fill in the questions at the end of each devotional.

6. Consider how the devotional, and the scriptures specifically, speak to your personal experiences. Can you relate to the story? Have you had similar experiences or feelings?

As you move along through the daily devotionals, you will find the common theme is this: everyday life. I will take you through the seasons, share some of my gardening exploits, relate stories from days past. I bet you never associated slugs with sin. Don't worry, you will! Whatever the theme, the connecting thread will be how to apply God's Word.

I will tell you up front-this book is NOT a highly intellectual study of the Bible. It is written in simple terms by a simple gal who simply loves Jesus! And my intent is to show how this amazing Savior can permeate every part of our lives, and more importantly, our hearts.

I am going out on a limb here and assume that, by considering this book, you have a desire to grow deeper in your relationship with Jesus. If so, you are in the right place. Welcome aboard!

**I do not profess to be a theologian, Bible scholar, or even a teacher. I am a student of the Word, just as you are. It is my hope and prayer that we will together glean beautiful nuggets of truth about our glorious Savior. At the end of the day, we will see that it all boils down to this fact:

It's All About Jesus!

So grab your Bible and let's get started!

FEARLESS LEVI
(Facing Our Fears)

Fear is an interesting thing. Sometimes real, sometimes totally irrational.

My dog Levi is a Corgi Beagle mix, with one ear that stands up, and one ear that flops down. He has big brown eyes and the sweetest disposition you will ever see in a dog. He puts on his tough-guy act whenever an uninvited dog happens to stroll past his territory. He will bravely stand on hind legs as he barks ferociously through the front window. Always at the ready to protect life and property!

That is, until a fly wanders into the house. Then suddenly he turns into the Cowardly Lion. Yep, my brave little guy is afraid of flies! As Levi lost his first owner, I will never know if he was stung by a bee, which may give reason for his fear.

When his radar detects a fly, he cowers in the bathroom or under the table. His upright ear is on high alert, turning this way and then the other, as he is listening for the telltale buzz of the enemy. When the coast is clear, he will dart across the room in stealth mode, braving the open space. He knows that makes him a target. He will not relax as long as that fly is buzzing around!

Then something interesting takes place. When I notice this is happening (and growing weary of the fly myself), I will get up and grab the fly swatter. "Come on, Levi. Let's go get that fly!" Suddenly, he has found his courage, and will follow behind me, head and tail up and chest out, as we search high and low together for the enemy. Safety in numbers, I guess! He will even snap at it when it dares to get too close.

After I finally get the little bugger, I have to make a show of it. I scoop it onto the fly swatter and ceremoniously toss it out the front door and shout, 'Yay, Levi! The fly is gone!" His tail starts to wag, and you can almost see him breathe a sigh of relief. It is safe to go out into the sun again! Or, in this case, the living room. (The back yard is still a work in progress. Just keep that back door open, and my path to safety clear, Mom!)

Oftentimes fear can be paralyzing. Especially when you have to face it alone. Ever notice when you are by yourself at night, the house seems to take on a life of its own? Noises occur that you wouldn't even pay attention to with other people around. God does not want us to be living in fear. So looking at His Word, how can we go about conquering this stronghold?

FIRST-RECOGNIZE GOD'S PRESENCE

"Have I not commanded you? Be strong and of good courage; do not be afraid, nor be dismayed, for the Lord your God is with you wherever you go." (Joshua 1:9) Understanding that God promises to be with us makes it a whole lot easier to be brave. There is comfort in knowing that He is right there beside us at all times!

"Yea, though I walk through the valley of the shadow of death, I will fear no evil; for You are with me; Your rod and Your staff, they comfort me." (Psalm 23:4) Jesus will give us comfort in the darkest night of the soul.

SECOND-SEEK HIM

"I sought the Lord, and He heard me, and delivered me from all my fears." (Psalm 34:4) If we seek Him, He will be faithful to answer our call.

"Whenever I am afraid, I will trust in You. In God (I will praise His Word), in God I have put my trust; I will not fear. What can flesh do to me?" (Psalm 56:3-4) God is bigger than anything man can attempt to do to us.

"When you pass through the waters, I will be with you; and through the rivers, they shall not overflow you. When you walk through the fire, you shall not be burned, nor shall the flame scorch you. For I am the Lord your God, the Holy One of Israel, your Savior..." (Isaiah 43:2-3) Isn't it comforting to know that no matter what we are going through, He will be right there beside us?

FINALLY-TRUST HIM

"So do not fear, for I am with you; do not be dismayed, for I am your God. I will strengthen you and help you; I will uphold you with my righteous right hand." (Isaiah 41:10) What a beautiful picture of God holding me and strengthening me.

"In the multitude of my anxieties within me, Your comforts delight my soul." (Psalm 94:19) He promises peace in our soul when we seek Him.

"The Lord is my light and my salvation; whom shall I fear? The Lord is the strength of my life; of whom shall I be afraid?" (Psalm 27:1) God's light will outshine any fear. He will overpower any other stronghold in our lives.

As you can see, God's promises are pretty strong. If you put all these scriptures together, it is clear that God promises He will always be there with us, walking right beside us. He will give us the courage and strength to get through the trial.

Getting back to Levi. His fear is irrational. But as his protector, I know that he is going to be ok. He trusts me to take care of him. God is the same way. And He is much more powerful. He can take what seems like giants in our eyes and reduce them down to pesky little flies.

When we are walking with Jesus, we have nothing to fear. We are safe in His loving and protective arms. He is our Comforter, Protector, and Shield. We can face anything that life throws at us. All we have to do is call out to Him!

7

REFLECTION TIME

What fear or fears are you facing today?

_____

_____

_____

_____

_____

_____

Meditate on the above scriptures. How do they speak to your heart?

_____

_____

_____

_____

_____

Write out a prayer, asking Jesus to help you face your fear.

_____

_____

_____

_____

_____

_____

~~~~~~~

Thank you, Lord Jesus, for Your promises. Your Word says that we have nothing to fear, because You are with us. You will walk side by side with us, guiding us and protecting us. Thank you for slaying the giants in our lives, because to You, they ARE just pesky little flies. Help us to be strong and bold as we navigate through this life. In Your name we pray, AMEN!

**NOTE: After this writing, Levi crossed over the "Rainbow Bridge" …where there are no flies, nor anything else to be afraid of! (May 22, 2019) You will be missed, little guy!

∿ ADDITIONAL NOTES ∿

I HAVE FAITH...SORT OF
(Strengthening Our Faith)

I don't know about you, but I am the type of person who needs to know what's going on. I don't like being kept in the dark. My strategy is to have a well-thought-out plan before I embark on something. Spontaneity is not part of my character. Sure, I like to do things on the spur of the moment, but let's plan it out a little bit first, ok?

Some people thrive on the adventure. Let's throw caution to the wind and see where life takes us. Maybe they have more confidence; perhaps they're a little crazy. I would never do well in a temp job where you are somewhere new every day. I hate feeling like I don't know what I am doing.

It would be nice if God would tell us what He has planned before we start. Ok, we are going to do step one, then step two, and so on until the job is complete. Nope. Not only does He not share ahead of time what He wants us to do, but He also holds back on the timing of it. Lord is this going to happen next week, or next year....

I think if He told all we needed to know up front, a few things would probably happen. First, we would get in there with our own ideas and muck everything up. We would rely on our own strength instead of seeking Him along the way. We might even refuse to do it because we know that some rather unpleasant things are going to happen along the way. Ignorance truly IS bliss sometimes.

Most importantly, I believe we would cease trusting in Him. To step out on faith can be scary. But if we fully trust Him, we don't have to be afraid. There are times-a lot of times actually- that God's actions don't make sense to us.

"'For My thoughts are not your thoughts, nor are your ways My ways' says the Lord. 'For as the heavens are higher than the earth, So are My ways higher than your ways, and My thoughts than your thoughts.'" (Isaiah 55:8-9). God's plans are so much bigger and better than we could ever design, and often times they simply don't make sense to us. Not yet, anyway!

~~~~~~~

Here are three different scenarios regarding faith:

TRUSTING THE UNKNOWN (Joshua Chapter 3)

In this story, the priests were carrying the Ark of the Covenant. They reached the Jordan river, which was at flood stage. When they reached the riverbank, God had the priests dip their toes in the Jordan river before He parted it so they could cross. He performed a miracle, but the priests had to step out, literally, in faith first. Did they question how they were going to get to the other side? We don't know; it doesn't say. I would suspect from a human standpoint that they were concerned. But they had to show faith before the miracle would occur.

HE KNEW, BUT WENT ANYWAY (Acts Ch 9:10-16, 2 Corinthians 11:22-29)

The apostle Paul, on the other hand, was told ahead of time what the cost would be to him personally to follow Jesus. God sent Ananias to tell him everything that would happen to him. Well, as you read Paul's description in 2 Corinthians of the physical sufferings he endured, you would probably agree that it must have taken a lot of conviction and courage to do what was laid out for him. Honestly, if I heard all of that, I don't know if I would be strong enough for the job. But Paul trusted his Savior that He would sustain him through every trial.

YOU CAN'T WALK ON WATER SITTING IN THE BOAT (Matthew 14:28-32)

In the new testament, Peter is an excellent example of stepping out in faith. Literally. The boys are out fishing, when suddenly a fierce storm begins. The apostles are very afraid. Then Jesus literally walks on the water to the boat. Here is where we pick up the story:

"Peter answered Him and said, 'Lord, if it is You, command me to come to You on the water.' So He said, 'Come.' And when Peter had come down out of the boat, he walked on the water to go to Jesus. But when he saw that the wind was boisterous, he was afraid; and beginning to sink he cried out, saying, 'Lord, save me!' And immediately Jesus stretched out His hand and caught him, and said to him, 'O you of little faith, why did you doubt?' And when they got into the boat, the wind ceased."

What's interesting about this story is it that it shows both sides of Peter. First there is the courageous, bold man who was full of trust for His Lord. Then there's the worldly Peter who takes his eyes off Jesus and gets into his own head, so to speak. He sees the tumult around him, panics, forgets about Jesus and starts to sink like a rock. His faith took him out on the water, but his flesh almost took him under.

Faith is a beautiful and scary part of our walk with Jesus. Most of the time, He will only show us what we need now, today. He knows our weak flesh. Sometimes, that faith will be tested and stretched so that we can grow it. Like a muscle, it needs to be used to get stronger. Other times we can get overconfident, and end up boasting in ourselves, or get ahead of the Lord.

When God reveals only enough light for us to see the step in front of us or asks us to dip our toes in the water first, we need to embrace our faith, cling to Him and trust that He will get us to the other side. And if we are going to let Jesus drive the car, we need to stop grabbing the wheel from Him. Amen?

REFLECTION TIME

Think of a time when you had to rely on your faith to see you through a situation. How were you able to navigate through it?

_____

_____

_____

_____

_____

_____

_____

Have you had a "Peter moment" in your life, where you were full of faith, then took your eyes off Jesus? What was that experience like, and what would you do differently?

_____

_____

_____

_____

_____

_____

_____

Write a prayer asking God to continue to grow your faith, and to keep you strong when you need to use it.

_____

_____

_____

_____

_____

_____

_____

Dear Father: Thank you that we can trust and rest in Your promise to be faithful even when we are not. Help us to keep our eyes on You, trusting You every step of the way. We know that You will always get us to the other side! In Jesus name, Amen!

~~ ADDITIONAL NOTES ~~

~~ DAY 3 ~~

THE POWER OF PRAYER
(Our Strongest Weapon)

Did you know that prayer is the most potent weapon in the Christian's arsenal? It has the power to move mountains! If you have ever been to a prayer meeting, no doubt you have discovered they can be amazing! People are just pouring out their hearts to the Savior, lifting up the heavy burdens they are carrying. Let me tell you, a women's prayer group is something else!

I remember when I was a newbie Christian. The thought of praying out loud with other people terrified me! We would sit in a circle, taking turns praying on whatever the issue was. As I was waiting for my turn, I would be frantically running requests through my head. I will ask for this or that. Sure enough, just when I had my thoughts together, someone stole my ideas! Great. What do I say now? And I always felt like I was tripping over my own tongue. It never failed-the person praying right before me prayed like they swallowed a bible, quoting every scripture they ever knew, adding to my angst. But as they say, practice makes perfect. Or at least it makes you better. With time, I slowly lost my fear of public praying, and rather than being preoccupied with my "script", I allowed the Holy Spirit to guide my words. Hopefully, they have been effective prayers.

~~~~~~

Since prayer is such a powerful weapon, why don't we utilize it more? It bothers me when people say, "There's nothing else I can do. All that's left is prayer." What??? Prayer should and *must* be our first response to any situation. Sometimes it should be our only course of action. Too often we try to fix a situation and get in God's way.

WHY WE SHOULD PRAY

We are instructed to pray. When Jesus gave the disciples the model on prayer in Matthew 6, He said "when" you pray, not "If".

"And they continued steadfastly in the apostles' doctrine and fellowship, in the breaking of bread, and in prayers." (Acts2:42) It was part of the apostle's creed when the church was established in Acts.

"Pray without ceasing…for this is the will of God." (1 Thessalonians 5:17-18). It doesn't mean 24/7, but we are to have that attitude of prayer, in constant communion with the Lord.

"Be anxious for nothing, but in everything by prayer and supplication, with thanksgiving, let your requests be made known to God; and the peace of God, which surpasses all understanding, will guard your hearts and minds through Christ Jesus." (Philippians 4:6-7) Giving everything over to God will give us peace above what we can humanly understand.

UNANSWERED PRAYERS

"…you do not have because you do not ask. You ask and do not receive, because you ask amiss, that you may spend it on your pleasures." (James 4:2-3) Sometimes we just don't bother to seek the Lord; oftentimes we are praying for selfish motives.

"But your iniquities have separated you from your God; and your sins have hidden His face from you, so that He will not hear." (Isaiah 59:2). Unconfessed sin is a barrier between God and us. Remember, He cannot look upon sin.

"Now this is the confidence that we have in Him, that if we ask anything according to His will, He hears us. And if we know that He hears us, whatever we ask, we know that we have the petitions that we have asked of Him." (1 John 5:14) We must be in His will. Because if we aren't, then our motives are going to be selfish and contrary to what God has for us. Jesus always prayed in His Father's will.

You might think, well I don't pray very well. Why would He listen to me? Trust me; God is not impressed with long, deep theological prayers. Jesus criticized the hypocrites for just that:

"And when you pray, you shall not be like the hypocrites. For they love to pray standing in the synagogues and on the corners of the streets, that they may be seen by men. Assuredly, I say to you, they have their reward. But you, when you pray, go into your room, and when you have shut your door, pray to your Father who is in the secret place; and your Father who sees in secret will reward you openly. And when you pray, do not use vain repetitions as the heathen do. For they think that they will be heard for their many words." (Matthew 6:5-7) No comment needed here!

Here is Paul's exhortation to Timothy regarding prayer:

"Therefore I exhort first of all that supplications, prayers, intercessions, and giving of thanks be made for all men, for kings and all who are in authority, that we may lead a quiet and peaceable life in all godliness and reverence. For this is good and acceptable in the sight of God our Savior, who desires all men to be saved and to come to the knowledge of the truth. For there is one God and one Mediator between God and men, the Man Christ Jesus." (1 Timothy 2:1-5)

We need to remember that we are praying to God. Not to saints, not to Mary, but to our Heavenly Father. Jesus is the only intercessor we need. He said Himself, *"I am the Way, the Truth, and the Life. No one can come to the Father except through Me."* (John 14:6). This direct access to the throne came about when Jesus declared, *"It is finished!"* from the cross. *"And Jesus cried out again with a loud voice and yielded up His spirit. Then, behold, the veil of the temple was torn in two from top to bottom..."* (Matthew 27:50-51) Hallelujah!

~~~~~~~

Jesus longs to hear from you. Prayers of thanksgiving, intercession, forgiveness. He cares about anything and everything that is on your heart. Don't worry about how you may sound. It is sweet music to Him! Keeping that conduit of communication open to Him is essential. Set

17

aside a specific time of prayer. Morning prayer is an excellent way to start the day off. I heard a pastor once say that beginning your day without talking with the Lord is like a football coach not preparing for the game, then wondering afterward why the team lost. So start the day off with your marching orders from Jesus. It really will make a difference in your day. It's nice to know that Someone has your back!

REFLECTION TIME

How would you describe your prayer life?

_____

_____

_____

_____

_____

_____

What are some ways you can strengthen your prayer time with Jesus?

_____

_____

_____

_____

_____

_____

Write out a prayer, asking God to help you pray for whatever is on your heart. Become an intercessor for others. And watch the power of your prayer life explode!

_____

_____

_____

_____

_____

_____

~~~~~~~

Thank You Heavenly Father, for the privilege of being able to come boldly to the throne of grace. Thank You that through the death and resurrection of Your Son, we have direct access to You. Help us to use this powerful weapon for the glory of Your Kingdom. In Jesus name, Amen!

~~ DAY 4 ~~

A JOYFUL NOISE
(The Heart of Worship)

When I lived in Southern California, I attended a large church. Worship music was an integral part of the service. We had a full-on band, with multiple guitars, drums, and keyboards. The music was loud in volume, so it was hard to hear others singing, except for one certain worshipper.

There was this dear lady who sat across the aisle and up a few rows. She sang with total abandon. Loud, slightly off-key, and often one or two words ahead or behind the worship team. My initial reaction was, "Where is that noise coming from??" But the heavenly perspective is totally different. I picture Jesus sitting there, enjoying the congregation's voices lifted up in praise to Him. Then He pauses, and says, "Wait a minute. Something's off a bit. It sounds like a clanging cymbal. It's like a clanging cymbal of criticism. And it's coming from, let's see, over there on the right somewhere." Busted! That would be me. Forgive me Lord, and may I worship with the same abandon as your precious daughter across the aisle. But since I am well aware of my vocal limitations, I will confine my abandon to the heart, which is where Jesus is looking anyway! From that day on, I came to enjoy the sweetness of this lady.

~~~~~~~~

On the other hand, some people don't see the importance of worship music. They look at it as the coming attractions at a movie theatre. They make it a habit to come in late during the music, disrupting other worshippers. Or just as bad, they stand there yapping back and forth during the songs. It's not the warm-up act, folks!

This time should be considered sacred. It is a vital part of the service. Worship music is designed to prepare our hearts to hear and receive what God has to say through the teaching of His Word. It is a time to praise the Lord, to give back to Him.

There are many forms of worship. The Bible speaks of singing psalms and praise; there is also worship through our words. Even our deeds can be used to worship the Lord.

SONGS OF PRAISE

"Oh, give thanks to the Lord! Call upon His name; make known His deeds among the peoples! Sing to Him, sing psalms to Him; talk of all His wondrous works! Glory in His holy name; let the hearts of those rejoice who seek the Lord!" (1 Chronicles 16:8-10). This passage makes me want to get up and shout His name!

"Praise Him with the timbrel and dance; Praise Him with stringed instruments and flutes!" (Psalm 150:4) Musical instruments were used extensively in the Old Testament to praise the Lord. David invented some of them. The instruments were the harp, lute, lyre, cymbal, tambourine, and horn. (Psalm 150:3-5)

"Make a joyful shout to the Lord, all you lands! Serve the Lord with gladness; come before His presence with singing." (Psalm 100:1) God listens to the music that we create in our heart. If we are praising the Lord, then it is a sweet sound. If there is bitterness, strife, etc. then it is a clanging cymbal.

"Praise the Lord, for the Lord is good; Sing praises to His name, for it is pleasant." (Psalm 135:3) A heartfelt praise song is sweet to the soul.

WORDS OF PRAISE

"Therefore by Him let us continually offer the sacrifice of praise to God, that is, the fruit of our lips, giving thanks to His name." (Hebrews 13:15). Our hearts should always be in a state of thanksgiving, which will then translate to words of praise.

21

"I will praise You, O Lord my God, with all my heart, and I will glorify Your name forevermore." (Psalm 86:12) He is indeed worthy of all praise, every day.

"And my tongue shall speak of Your righteousness and of Your praise all the day long." (Psalm 35:28) Imagine how much smoother our day would go if we focused on the goodness of the Lord.

"I will bless the Lord at all times; His praise shall continually be in my mouth." (Psalm 34:1) If there are praises in your mouth, then there's no room for the negative stuff!

PRAISE THROUGH DEEDS

"And whatever you do in word or deed, do all in the name of the Lord Jesus, giving thanks to God the Father through Him." (Colossians 3:17) If we conduct ourselves with the mindset that we are doing all things for the Lord, no matter what it is, then we are praising His name. We will also do a better job!

"If you love Me, keep My commandments." (John 14:15) Part of praise and worship is to be in obedience to the Lord.

"Therefore, whether you eat or drink, or whatever you do, do all to the glory of God." (1 Corinthians 10:31) We need to stay mindful of how we behave. Does it honor God, or tear Him down?

"I beseech you therefore, brethren, by the mercies of God, that you present your bodies a living sacrifice, holy, acceptable to God, which is your reasonable service." (Romans 12:1) As Christians, we are to live a life that is pleasing to God. We do not want to present corrupted sacrifices.

As we have learned from the scriptures, worship and praise can take on many forms. Whether it be in singing, words or actions, we want our praise to be genuine and worthy of the name of Jesus. He deserves no less than our best. But we need to be walking the walk, not just talking it. Amen?

REFLECTION TIME

How would you describe your worship life? Is it thriving, or is it on life-support?

_____

_____

_____

_____

_____

_____

_____

In what ways can you develop a deeper expression of worship to your Lord?

_____

_____

_____

_____

_____

_____

_____

Write a prayer asking God to help you in this area.

_____

_____

_____

_____

_____

_____

_____

Thank you, Jesus, that You love to hear from our hearts. I pray that it is a pleasing sound to You. Forgive us when we start hitting those sour notes, grumbling, and murmuring. Help us to keep our minds stayed on You. In Your precious name, Amen!

~ ADDITIONAL NOTES ~

~~ DAY 5 ~~

STUCK IN THE MUCK
(Jesus Is the Rock)

Rainy days are rejuvenating. They clear the air, water our lawns, and bring an all-around freshness to our surroundings. Prolonged rain or snow, on the other hand, can make for a muddy mess.

Have you ever had this experience? You're sloshing around in your soggy yard. You go to take a step, and shlppp! There goes your shoe! Right off your foot and sucked into the miry mirk. I had this happen to me the other day. I was trying to walk through the freshly fallen snow drift in my backyard. Granted I was wearing my everyday slip-ons. Hey, I am from Southern California! Not prepared for this. At least I wasn't wearing flip flops! Anyway, I stood there, one foot still in the snow, the other hovering above it, shoeless. I pondered my predicament. The dry, solid patio was too far away for me to step over onto it. Then there was the issue of my other foot. Will I lose that shoe as well? As I stood there like a flamingo, I considered my choices. The only option I could think of was to continue toward the patio, probably losing my other shoe as well. Seeing that as my only way out, I trekked over to the patio. Sure enough, shoe #2 joined the party. Grrr....

Finally making it to the clear cement with cold feet and sopping wet socks, I lamented my bad fortunes. I went into the house, changed my socks and while I thawed out my tootsies, I thought about my favorite shoes, buried alive. I guess I could retrieve them in the Spring thaw.... then I chastised myself for not having galoshes. Hindsight is 20/20. I should have had them in the first place, and I could have prevented this whole ordeal. A trip to the shoe store has just been added to my errand list!

25

The Bible talks about the miry clay. The ordeal that gets us "stuck". As always, Jesus is at the ready, willing and able to pull us out of our muck and mire. Ponder these verses:

"PIT" SURVIVORS

"He also brought me up out of a horrible pit, out of the miry clay, and set my feet upon a rock, and established my steps." (Psalm 40:2) Sometimes the "pits" in our lives are due to circumstances out of our control. A lost job, a loved one passing; basically, life happening. Oh, and then there are those self-induced pits. Usually caused by choosing to sin which then leads to a downfall.

~~~~~~~

The question is not, will I experience the miry clay, but how will I respond when I find myself in it? There are a couple of real pits mentioned in the Bible. Joseph found himself physically in a pit when his jealous brothers tossed him into one. What was his response?

"But as for you, you meant evil against me; but God meant it for good, in order to bring it about as it is this day, to save many people alive." (Genesis 50:20) Of course, he saw the outcome many years later, but he put his trust in God the entire time. And God had the perfect plan all along!

Then there's the story of the three boys Shadrach, Meshach, and Abed-Nego, who knew in advance they would be thrown into a fiery furnace if they didn't obey the king. Catch this response:

"If that is the case, our God whom we serve is able to deliver us from the burning fiery furnace, and He will deliver us from your hand, O king." (Daniel 3:17) They looked their trial square in the eye and faced it, knowing that God was with them. Their confidence and trust in their Lord did not waver based on their circumstances.

What is our response when we find ourselves in the pit? Do we throw a pity party? Woe is me, the world is against me, no one cares about me, if

God loves me, then why is this happening to me? Or, do we search the scriptures, seeking His promises?

COMFORTING PASSAGES

"And the Lord said, 'Here is a place by Me, and you shall stand on the rock.'" (Exodus 33:21) That gives me great comfort knowing that I can stand right next to my Savior.

"No one is holy like the Lord, for there is none besides You, nor is there any rock like our God." (1 Samuel 2:2) He is King of kings, Lord of Lords, Holy and Righteous are His names.

"Do not fear, nor be afraid; have I not told you from that time, and declared it? You are My witnesses. Is there a God besides Me? Indeed, there is no other Rock; I know not one." (Isaiah 44:8) God is the only Rock I need. No other "god" will suffice.

"And the rain descended, the floods came, and the winds blew and beat on that house; and it did not fall, for it was founded on the rock." (Matthew 7:25) He is the unfailing shelter in any storm that comes my way.

~~~~~~~~

In my little story earlier, the dry solid ground of the cement patio was my rock. I was on a firm foundation. Jesus is my Spiritual Rock. Keeping me, protecting me, and holding me near to Him. He's the shelter in my storm. I know that He will keep me from sinking. But like a man in quicksand, I need to stop struggling, quit the pity party and grab His outstretched Hand. And if I leave my shoes behind in the muck, that's ok. I think He can take care of that too!

REFLECTION TIME

Think of a time when you felt you were in a "pit"? What was your response to it?

_____

_____

_____

_____

_____

_____

_____

When you read that Jesus is our Rock, how does that give you comfort?

_____

_____

_____

_____

_____

_____

_____

Write out a prayer, thanking God for His steadfastness and to help you cling to Him in any storm.

_____

_____

_____

_____

_____

_____

_____

Thank you, Lord Jesus, that You are the Rock on which we stand. A solid beacon in the storm. Help us to praise You in advance for reaching out and pulling us out of the miry clay of life. In Your Name, Amen!

~~ ADDITIONAL NOTES ~~

~~ DAY 6 ~~

BUSY, BUSY, BUSY!
(Resting in Jesus)

Life has become so hectic these days. We live in a technological world. Things are designed to go faster, save time, streamline our work, increase our productivity. We want it fast, we want it now, and it needs to be efficient.

Do you remember the days of dial-up internet? Rotary phones? Pre-fast food restaurants? Looking things up in encyclopedias?? Nowadays, we can get information at the touch of a few keystrokes. And hey, we can even speak into our computers or phones so we don't have to take the time to type!

With all of this technology, we have become very impatient. In times past, when we would call someone on the phone and they weren't home, we would leave a message, and probably wait a few hours until they got home. Now we expect a reply to our texts right away. High-speed internet has replaced dial-up, and now we have super-fast DSL. Heaven forbid I should have to wait more than a few seconds for the information I am looking for to come up. I did a test. I searched Google for several topics. Instantly, usually less than half a second, hundreds of thousands of links came up. It took me longer to type the word! And of course, faxing and emailing is far superior to "snail mail".

You expect me to *wait* at the fast food restaurant? I want my food ready for me by the time I pull around to the second window. Oh, and I want it hot, and the order to be accurate. At some restaurants, you don't have to wait in line; you can order ahead, and it will be ready for you when you get there. Even better, have your sandwich delivered to you, so you don't have to stop to go out and get it. Or nuke your lunch made from some Frankenfood you purchased from the snack bar.

We seem to be losing touch with one another. It's easier to text than to chat on the phone. Social media has become far more interesting than engaging with one another at a restaurant table. Have you ever watched a group of teenagers crossing the street? They all have their heads bent down; eyes glued to their phones. I have to laugh because I saw a video of a young woman walking in the mall, so engrossed in her phone, that she walked right into the fountain and fell in! I felt bad for her, but it did give me a giggle. Actually, I think it was her reaction. She got out and just kept walking!

~~~~~~

So does this crazy, busy pace we are all wrapped up in make for a better lifestyle? Or has it just added to the stress and chaos of the rat race? Does working sixty hours a week to pay for all the gadgets and gizmos that are supposed to make our life easier make sense? Is there room for Jesus in all of this, or has He been pushed aside because there's no time to squeeze Him in? Have we forgotten how to slow down and enjoy His presence?

RESTING AT HIS FEET

"He makes me to lie down in green pastures; He leads me beside the still waters. He restores my soul…" (Psalm 23:2) What a beautiful picture of rest. Just sitting by the waters, being restored.

"Come to Me, all you who labor and are heavy laden, and I will give you rest." (Matthew 11:28) When we are tired and beaten down, He will renew and refresh us.

"Be still and know that I am God…" (Psalm 46:10) When everything is going crazy around you, stop and seek the Lord. Trust and know that He is God.

GOD'S PERSPECTIVE

"But this Man, after He had offered one sacrifice for sins forever, sat down at the right hand of God." (Hebrews 10:12) Even Jesus rested after completing His mission.

"But those who wait on the Lord shall renew their strength; They shall mount up with wings like eagles, they shall run and not be weary, they shall walk and not faint." (Isaiah 40:31) Sometimes we feel like we have hit the wall in this marathon race. But He will strengthen us for the journey.

"And He said to them, 'The Sabbath was made for man, and not man for the Sabbath. Therefore the Son of Man is also Lord of the Sabbath.'" (Mark 2:27) We need to set a day aside to rest and abide in Jesus. Put the work and the busyness aside and just sit at His feet.

~~~~~~~~

God is not calling us to run ourselves ragged. Even in ministry, we can get so busy doing His work, that we forget about Him. Here is a challenge for you. Take a day off and disconnect from the world. Turn off your phones, your computers, and all the gadgets. Grab your Bible, a cup of coffee and find a quiet place to rest. Just step back, enjoy what God has given you, stop striving for more, and embrace the love of Jesus. You will be renewed and refreshed, just like He promises!

REFLECTION TIME

Do you have a crazy, jampacked schedule? How have you allowed the busyness of your day crowd out your time with Jesus?

_____

_____

_____

_____

_____

_____

What are some ways that you can carve out some meaningful time with Jesus, making Him the priority of your day?

_____

_____

_____

_____

_____

_____

Write out a prayer, asking God for that extra measure of peace, and time for refreshing and renewal of your soul.

_____

_____

_____

_____

_____

_____

~~~~~~~

Thank you Lord, that you created these magnificent machines called the human body. But they were not designed to go non-stop. Help us to put aside the drive to achieve more and more at the expense of spending time with You. Help us to be still and know that You are God! In Your name, Amen!

CHOCOLATE-SINFULLY GOOD
(The Danger of Sin)

Ah, chocolate. Rich, gooey, decadent. God *must* have created this delectable delight. Man wouldn't be able to invent something so wonderful!

Chocolate comes in so many variations — dark, milk, white. Paired with caramel, hazelnut, orange; the list is endless. It was practically a national holiday for me when the chocolate industry declared that dark chocolate is actually GOOD for you. Oh, happy day!

When the holidays hit, oh my, I am in seventh heaven! The samples at Costco come out. It's a chocolate lover's delight. Especially at Christmas time. Lindor's chocolate truffles. I am drooling just thinking about them! I will let you in on a little secret. Not all demo ladies are alike. When they hand out the truffles, some are more generous than others. There's one lady there who will give you one and one only. Another lady, all I do is hold out my apron pocket, and she loads it up. SCORE!!! So it pays to scope them out.

Like anything, too much of a good thing is not healthy for you. Even dark chocolate has its limitations. It may taste wonderful going down, but too much of it can have some adverse side effects. Weight gain, sugar complications, and gastrointestinal issues are some of the problems it causes.

Sin is a lot like chocolate. It may be fun to indulge in, but there are consequences. But unlike chocolate, where moderation is okay, sin has no "safe" level. Sin in any form is a very serious issue with God. He has no tolerance for it at all.

HOW GOD FEELS ABOUT SIN

"But your iniquities have separated you from your God, and your sins have hidden His face from you so that He will not hear." (Isaiah 59:2) God cannot look upon sin. That's why when Jesus took the entire world's sin upon Himself on the cross, the Father had to forsake Him.

"Do not be deceived, God is not mocked; for whatever a man sows, that he will also reap." (Galatians 6:7) Sin comes with a hefty price tag. God sees all; we cannot hide from Him. We must be accountable.

"He who sins is of the devil, for the devil has sinned from the beginning. For this purpose, the Son of God was manifested, that He might destroy the works of the devil." (1 John 3:8) To be of the devil is disturbing indeed! Praise God that He can smash the enemy.

"Let no one say when he is tempted, 'I am tempted by God'; for God cannot be tempted by evil, nor does He Himself tempt anyone. But each one is tempted when he is drawn away by his own desires and enticed. Then, when desire has conceived, it gives birth to sin; and sin, when it is full-grown, brings forth death." (James 1:13-15) Temptation is at the root of all sin. We must keep it in check, resist it from the get-go before it gets ahold of us.

~~~~~~

When we think of sin, we automatically think of the "big" ones. Sins like murder, sexual immorality, stealing. The ten commandment ones. But did you know that God puts things like gossip, backbiting, and gluttony right in there with them? Check out Romans 1:28-32 for a list of sins. Very sobering.

When we dabble in sin, we are setting ourselves up for a mighty fall. Like potato chips, the first one just opens the door to eating the entire bag. Only this one time, you may say. But one time leads to a second time, then a third, and eventually you will find yourself in far deeper than you ever wanted to go. An illicit affair starts off with a not-so-innocent glance...

Fortunately, we have a loving and forgiving Father, who has made a way out. It was through Jesus, who paid the penalty with the shedding of His blood.

THE WAY OF ESCAPE

"No temptation has overtaken you except such as is common to man; but God is faithful, who will not allow you to be tempted beyond what you are able, but with the temptation will also make the way of escape, that you may be able to bear it." (1 Corinthians 10:13) We have a path of escape, and that path is Jesus!

"Therefore submit to God. Resist the devil, and he will flee from you." (James 4:7) If we seek God and resist the sin, Satan is neutralized.

"Be sober, be vigilant; because your adversary the devil walks about like a roaring lion, seeking whom he may devour." (1 Peter 5:8) We need to be watchful. Satan's sole purpose is to destroy us. It's an ongoing battle. But thankfully, we do not have to fight it on our own. We have Jesus as our advocate.

"My little children, these things I write to you, so that you may not sin. And if anyone sins, we have an Advocate with the Father, Jesus Christ the righteous. And He Himself is the propitiation for our sins, and not for ours only but also for the whole world." (1 John 2:1-2) Words of wisdom from the Apostle John. We need to be mindful, though, that God's forgiveness is not a license to continue to sin. Let's not turn this awesome gift into cheap grace.

Sin is a very serious business, with potentially dire consequences. We are human. There will be times when we will fall. But if we strive to live the life Jesus calls us to, seek His forgiveness when we do stumble and get back on track, we will have a life that is abundant and rich because we will be walking with Him! No amount of chocolate can top that!

REFLECTION TIME

We are all tempted by sin every single day. Think of a time that you indulged in that temptation. What was the outcome?

_____

_____

_____

_____

_____

_____

_____

Knowing that Jesus is our advocate, how does that give you strength to overcome or avoid sin?

_____

_____

_____

_____

_____

_____

_____

Write out a prayer asking for strength to resist the devil, and to draw closer to Jesus.

_____

_____

_____

_____

_____

_____

Dear Father: You know that we are weak, with feet of clay. We deal with sin on a daily basis. Please search our hearts and reveal to us how we have fallen short. Forgive us for our sins, and please help us to stay on the right path. Thank You that You have made a way for us to resist the devil, and to draw on Your strength to keep us out of trouble! In Your name, Amen!

~~ ADDITIONAL NOTES ~~

~ DAY 8 ~

JESUS IS MY PESTICIDE
(*Our Defense Against Sin*)

Although I am by far NOT a gardening expert, this ain't my first rodeo, folks. (Or would that be my first trip around the planter box!) We had a garden every summer when I was a kid. We planted corn, pumpkins, green beans, strawberries. My dad had concord grapes, and my mom planted boysenberries. Amazing cobblers and jam! We also had several fruit trees. Apricot, fig, peach, orange, and lemon. Oh my, those apricots were so good! I do remember one day when I indulged in a few too many. Let's just say I had the worst tummy ache ever!

It's so rewarding when you see the fruits of your labor. Nothing better than homegrown, that's for sure. But there's nothing more disheartening than to go out one day and find you have had uninvited guests munching on your plants. One time, I planted marigolds between tomato bushes because I was told they would deter bugs. So I spaced out six plants between the tomatoes and thought everything would be fine. Ha! I went out to peruse my garden one morning, only to find every single marigold plant chomped down to just sticks! So much for that! So tell me, what do I plant to protect the marigolds??

~~~~~~~

One of the things gardeners love about this whole process is getting in the dirt. Feeling the warm earth, cultivating it, creating something beautiful in it. That's all well and good, but there's a downside to this. I freely admit that when it comes to creepy crawlies, I am a total girly-girl. I hate worms, snails, aphids, but above all… those horrid SLUGS! They gross me out. They are like overgrown snails without the house on top. And let me tell you, this past summer, these disgusting critters practically overran my little garden! They get down there in the wet grass, slither

39

around, waiting in the dark for their opportunity to take out your innocent lettuce leaves. They're like cockroaches. If you see one, you know you have more.

One day last summer, we decided to start fighting back. We don't use pesticides, so we had to attack the front line one-on-one. What I mean by that, is using a shovel, scooping them up and putting them in a plastic bag. This whole idea just gave me the willies. The first few made me very squeamish. But after a while, I started getting angry. How dare they attack my plants?? I started scooping them up with a vengeance. YOU WILL NOT PREVAIL was my battle cry!

I am reminded of the movie "Gone with the Wind". Halfway through, Scarlett O'Hara, our heroine, has been scrounging for food for her family in the war-torn plantation field. After a momentary breakdown, she pulls herself up by her petticoats, with a withered turnip clutched in her hand. She vows she will not be defeated. She stands in determination with her turnip held to the sky, declaring "As God is my witness, I'll never be hungry again!"

I know, it's a little dramatic for my slug issue, but I could relate to her resolve. You will not take what is mine!

~~~~~~

We have an enemy, called Satan, who is a lot like that. He lurks in the darkness, like a slithering, slimy slug. His sole purpose is to take us down. If we don't keep our guard up, he will devour us.

2 DIFFERENT OUTCOMES VS. SATAN

"The thief does not come except to steal, and to kill, and to destroy." (John 10:10) Remember in the garden of Eden when the serpent came to Eve and deceived her? See what fallout that has had over the years?? He appealed to her flesh and was victorious.

On the other hand, when Satan tried to tempt Jesus in the wilderness, there was a different response. Although Jesus had been fasting for 40 days and was weak, He was still able to withstand the wiles of the devil. Satan tried to appeal to his worldly need for food. But Jesus answered him, saying, *"It is written, 'Man shall not live by bread alone, but by every word of God.'"* (Luke 4:4)

~~~~~~

Getting back to my slugs. They are a lot like sin. Left unchecked, they will destroy everything in their path. I need to be proactive. But I can't do it in my own strength. I will get overwhelmed.

We are in a spiritual battle. Much more significant than the slugs in my garden. We have a powerful adversary. But we have a greater advocate In Jesus Christ. He is our strength, our fortress, the "pesticide" in the gardens of our souls… (sorry…!)

JESUS GIVES US THE VICTORY

"The sting of death is sin, and the strength of sin is the law. But thanks be to God, who gives us the victory through our Lord Jesus Christ." (1 Corinthians 15:56-57) Through Jesus, we can overcome anything Satan tries to throw at us.

"Yet in all these things we are more than conquerors through Him who loved us." (Romans 8:37). With Jesus, we are not only victorious, but we are *overwhelmingly* victorious. The enemy doesn't stand a chance!

"…He who is in you is greater than he who is in the world." (1 John 4:4) It has been said that we are no match for Satan, but Satan is no match for Jesus. But we do need to keep our guard up, our spiritual eyes open, stay focused on Jesus so sin and Satan cannot get a foothold. Then we can and will be victorious!

REFLECTION TIME

Search your heart. Is there a time when sin "snuck" up on you? How might have you prevented it from happening?

_____
_____
_____
_____
_____
_____
_____

When you think about Jesus being greater in us than Satan is in the world, how does that give you comfort?

_____
_____
_____
_____
_____
_____

Write out a prayer thanking Jesus that He is your advocate and ask for protection against sin and the wiles of the devil.

_____
_____
_____
_____
_____
_____
_____

Thank you Jesus, that You are our great Advocate. Help us to be strong in You, and to recognize ahead of time when sin is lurking at our door. Draw us close to You and protect us. Thank you, Jesus. In Your precious name, Amen!

~~ ADDITIONAL NOTES ~~

~~ DAY 9 ~~

EVERLASTING HOPE

(Hope in Jesus)

Fall is almost here. I love the refreshing crispness that permeates the air. The shadows are getting longer and softer. Nature arrays itself in beautifully vibrant reds, golds, and oranges. And when there is a backdrop of the deep evergreen trees found in the Pacific Northwest, it is a sight to behold!

Then comes the fall events. When I lived in Southern California, we would make our annual day trip up to this little mountain town called Oak Glen. We would trek our way out to the orchards and pick a basket or two of apples, then tromp through the pumpkin patches and pluck the pumpkins right off the vine. I always looked for one that had the gnarliest stem! Then we would stroll through the village checking out the fall festivities while sipping on apple cider. Usually, we would not be able to resist the enticing smells drifting out of the bakery. Yummy! There was also a crisp coolness in the air, which added to the fall atmosphere. Autumn is my favorite time of the year. Where I live here in Washington, you only have to drive about 10 minutes to get to the farms.

There is another annual ritual that takes place right about now. It's the beginning of football season. The fanatics awaken from their slumber. Sunday worship takes on a whole new meaning! (But now it's Monday night, Thursday night, Saturday night, etc. etc. etc.)

Hope springs eternal. Will this be the season that my team finally makes it to the Superbowl? Will the new quarterback be the savior we have been seeking? On opening day, the playing field is level. Every team has an equal chance. Fans will flock in droves with their team colors painted on their faces, wearing their favorite player's number on their jerseys.

Some people will even fly all over the country to follow their team. They are known as "The 12th Man".

Sadly, week by week, the pack starts to separate into the contenders and the "also-rans." Hope starts to fade, and thoughts of "maybe next year" take root.

This hope, like all worldly things, will eventually die. Things of this world are temporal. Placing faith in people, dreams, or ideas will usually end up in the trash heap, leaving us disappointed, disillusioned, and empty.

~~~~~~

The Bible speaks of an entirely different kind of hope. While the hope of man is based on what might happen, or for a desire of a specific outcome, God uses it as a certainty, with eternal value.

What is the Biblical definition of hope? It is the confident assurance we have that is built on the solid foundation of Jesus Christ. It doesn't waver or diminish based on circumstances. Why? Because *He* doesn't waver. Jesus is unchangeable. There is no shadow of turning with Him. Here are some scriptures to ponder:

HOPE SUPPLIED BY THE LORD

"Now may the God of hope fill you with all joy and peace in believing, that you may abound in hope by the power of the Holy Spirit." (Romans 15:13) God doesn't give hope. He IS hope. We can have joy and peace in every circumstance because we have been given eternal hope through the Holy Spirit. Unlike the football game, where our dream of victory will die when the team loses (adverse outcome), the confidence we have in Jesus will sustain us through the difficult time.

"Blessed be the God and Father of our Lord Jesus Christ, who according to His abundant mercy has begotten us again to a living hope through the resurrection of Jesus Christ from the dead." (1 Peter 1:3) What a glorious promise! Our hope is alive, because of the redemptive work Jesus did on the cross and His resurrection.

45

WE ARE THE BENEFACTORS OF THE LIVING HOPE:

"Blessed is the man who trusts in the Lord, And whose hope is the Lord." (Jeremiah 17:7) When we hope in the Lord, we can rejoice in the benefits from God, and know that Jesus is coming back soon for us!

"But I do not want you to be ignorant, brethren, concerning those who have fallen asleep, lest you sorrow as others who have no hope. For if we believe that Jesus died and rose again, even so, God will bring with Him those who sleep in Jesus." (1 Thessalonians 4:13-14) I love this passage because it describes the hope that believers in Christ have when our loved ones pass away (sleep here refers to death). We may sorrow, but we know we will see them again if they have put their trust in Jesus.

"Be of good courage, and He shall strengthen your heart, all you who hope in the Lord." (Psalm 21:34) We need to remember that through whatever trials we may have, the hope and faith we have in Jesus will strengthen and sustain us, no matter the outcome.

~~~~~~

To sum it all up, man's version of hope relies on successful circumstances. It will die if those circumstances don't come to pass. And it can change at the drop of a hat. God's version of hope as demonstrated in the Bible, is infallible, unfailing, eternal, and comforting when everything around us is falling apart. No matter what happens, God is still on the throne, and we are still His children if we have faith and belief in His Son, Jesus Christ.

Don't let the world rob you of this hope!

REFLECTION TIME

Ponder the scriptures above. How would you describe the difference between Biblical hope and worldly hope?

_____

_____

_____

_____

_____

_____

_____

Think of a time when you felt hopeless in a situation. How would the promises of God comfort you?

_____

_____

_____

_____

_____

_____

_____

Write a prayer asking God to strengthen your heart and to give you comfort when you are feeling hopeless or frightened.

_____

_____

_____

_____

_____

_____

_____

Dear Heavenly Father: Thank You for Your gift of eternal Hope and that we do not have to rely on our own strength to see us through the trials in our lives. Please bring into remembrance Your Word when we are faced with an overwhelming situation. Help us to see You as The Light IN the tunnel, not just at the end! In Your precious name, Amen.

~~ ADDITIONAL NOTES ~~

~~ DAY 10 ~~

FREE AS A BUTTERFLY

(A New Creation)

One of my favorite creations of God's is butterflies, with beautiful colors and intricate patterns on their wings. They flutter here and there, with total freedom. My mom had this huge pecan tree in her backyard, which we snuck over the Tennessee border when the tree was tiny (But that's a story for another time!). I would sit out there enjoying the cool shade, and sooner or later, this monarch butterfly would come along and land on my propped-up foot. It would rest there for a few moments before moving onto other destinations. Our brief visits happened a few times. A special treat from the Lord!

Many years earlier, when I was a child, we had a lantana bush. It attracted small butterflies. I would try to catch them by grasping the wings when they were closed together. A gold-like powdery "dust" remained on my fingertips. I imagine it was not beneficial for the little creatures. I remember taking empty coffee cans and poking holes in the plastic lids. I placed some grass in the container, and put my little butterfly inside, thinking this would be enough to keep it alive. I was always sad when I looked in my can the next day and saw that the little guy had expired. I didn't understand that it couldn't survive in those conditions.

Butterflies are a symbol of new life. They are born out of a cocoon that was initially formed by a caterpillar. It is a fascinating process. The caterpillar will eventually go through metamorphosis and emerge from the cocoon as a butterfly. The caterpillar has become a beautiful new creation.

49

God is in the business of turning us into new creations. He takes these old, broken down bodies and turns them into beautiful, vibrant vessels. This spiritual metamorphosis occurs because of His love for us, and His desire to conform us to His image.

A NEW CREATION

"Therefore, if anyone is in Christ, he is a new creation; old things have passed away; behold, all things have become new." (2 Corinthians 5:17) We have been forgiven of all our past sins. They are now dead. He has given us a fresh start with clean hands and pure hearts.

"Do not remember the former things, nor consider the things of old. Behold, I will do a new thing. Now it shall spring forth; shall you not know it? I will even make a road in the wilderness and rivers in the desert." (Isaiah 43:18-19) When we become children of God, we need to let go of the past and embrace our new lives as we walk with our Father.

"But we all, with unveiled face, beholding as in a mirror the glory of the Lord, are being transformed into the same image from glory to glory, just as by the Spirit of the Lord." (2 Corinthians 3:18) This Christian life is a constant work in progress. But as we grow in our knowledge and love for Him, we will take on more and more of His characteristics.

THE OUTCOME

"I have been crucified with Christ; it is no longer I who live, but Christ lives in me; and the life which I now live in the flesh I live by faith in the Son of God, who loved me and gave Himself for me." (Galatians 2:20) Upon receiving Jesus as our Lord and Savior, we have died to the old flesh nature. Christ is now abiding in us, and we should desire to live as one with Him.

"Then I will give them one heart, and I will put a new spirit within them, and take the stony heart out of their flesh, and give them a heart of flesh, so that they may walk in My statutes and keep My judgments and do them; and they shall be My people, and I will be their God." (Ezekiel 11:19-20) Isn't it awesome that He can take our cold, dead

hearts and turn them into warm, loving, alive hearts? Then we will be able to love and obey Him. I don't think we can do it otherwise.

"Therefore we were buried with Him through baptism into death, that just as Christ was raised from the dead by the glory of the Father, even so, we also should walk in newness of life." (Romans 6:4) Baptism represents this newness. When we are submerged into the water, we are burying the old, sin-filled life. When we come up from the water, it represents a spiritual rebirth. All things are new!

~~~~~~~

As you can see, the transformation we undergo when we become believers in Christ is much like the beginnings of a butterfly. The old flesh that is our sinful nature, disbelieving ways and flat-out rejection of Jesus can be like the caterpillar in the cocoon. But as we receive Jesus, we are being transformed into a new creation. As the butterfly breaks free from the cocoon, it will fly in freedom and newness. When we receive Jesus, we can let go of the chains that have kept us bound in sin, which can be represented by the cocoon. No longer are we prisoners of our sinful past. We are new creations, abiding in Jesus, and He is abiding in us. *"Therefore if the Son makes you free, you shall be free indeed."* (John 8:36)

The choice is yours. Do you want to be a caterpillar trapped in a life of sin and misery, or do you want to be a new creation, safely abiding in the loving arms of Jesus?

REFLECTION TIME

Has there been a time when you felt trapped like the caterpillar in the cocoon, needing or waiting for a spiritual breakthrough? Share your thoughts below.

_____

_____

_____

_____

_____

_____

_____

How did you find your way to Jesus through the experience?

_____

_____

_____

_____

_____

_____

_____

Write out a prayer, asking God to reveal any remnants of your old cocoon, and to show you how to have complete victory and freedom in Him.

_____

_____

_____

_____

_____

_____

_____

Dear Heavenly Father: Thank You that You love us so much, that You want to free us from all shackles and chains that are holding us back from a complete life with You. We ask that You continue to refine, shape and mold us into Your beautiful image. In Your Name, Amen!

~~ ADDITIONAL NOTES ~~

~~ DAY 11 ~~

A ROYAL VISIT
(Humility)

I have worked in corporate retail for most of the past 25 years. Each store has an internal chain of command. It starts with the store manager, then assistant manager, department managers, and so on down the food chain. Then there is the upper corporate management: district, regional, vice president, CEO. You can always tell when there is a corporate "walk-through" scheduled. Everyone is in a panic, and the tension in the air is so thick you can cut it with a knife. You would think that they were expecting a visit from the pope, the president and the queen of England all together! People are scurrying around checking this, scrubbing that, trying to make it perfect for this visit.

I remember those corporate visits at one company where I once worked. Oh, my! I got a kick out of watching the procession. All the managers followed behind the regional manager, looking like his entourage, with notebooks in hand; ready to write down every suggestion or critique he made. If he walked across the department, they all trailed behind him. If he turned around and walked the other way, they all did too, like little soldiers. Oh, and the facade everyone put on! Laughing at all his jokes, being friendly to everyone whom they usually didn't give a second glance. It was quite entertaining sometimes. After the corporate bigwigs were gone, everyone breathed a sigh of relief. It's funny how we treat the "upper echelons" better than we treat our peers. We act like they are demi-gods or something. Oh, and don't get me started on celebrities, who are fawned over and ogled, put up on a pedestal just because they are famous. News flash-we are all the same! They may be better known, but that doesn't make them better.

Humility is an essential topic in the Bible. Jesus set an example of the ultimate act of humility. Check this out:

"And being found in appearance as a man, He humbled Himself and became obedient to the point of death, even the death of the cross." (Philippians 2:8) This was the Son of God we are talking about here! He left His heavenly home, became a man, and was shamed, beaten and crucified on the cross. Why? So people could spit in His face, and blaspheme His name?? NO! So we could be forgiven of all our filthy unrighteousness.

God places a high priority on humility in man as well. He is not impressed with self-important attitudes.

GOD'S THOUGHTS TOWARD HUMILITY AND PRIDE:

"...Listen, my beloved brethren: Has God not chosen the poor of this world to be rich in faith and heirs of the kingdom which He promised to those who love Him? But you have dishonored the poor man. Do not the rich oppress you and drag you into the courts? Do they not blaspheme that noble name by which you are called?" (James 2:5-7) God is not a respecter of position or person. We are all equal in His eyes.

"Therefore, whoever humbles himself as this little child is the greatest in the kingdom of heaven." (Matthew 18:4) There's nothing more precious than the pure innocence of a child.

"For everyone who exalts himself will be humbled, and he who humbles himself will be exalted." (Luke 18:14) This is so contrary to worldly thinking!

"...If anyone desires to be first, he shall be last of all and servant of all." (Mark 9:35) Get to the back of the line, buddy!

"But He gives more grace. Therefore, He says 'God resists the proud, but gives grace to the humble.'" (James 4:6) God does not like pride.

OUR MARCHING ORDERS

"Be of the same mind toward one another. Do not set your mind on high things but associate with the humble. Do not be wise in your own opinion." (Romans 12:16) Oh, how we need to get over ourselves!

"Humble yourselves in the sight of the Lord, and He will lift you up." (James 4:10) All the way to heaven!

"Then Jesus called a little child to Him, set him in the midst of them, and said, 'Assuredly, I say to you, unless you are converted and become as little children, you will by no means enter the kingdom of heaven. Therefore whoever humbles himself as this little child is the greatest in the kingdom of heaven.'" (Matthew 18:2-4) Little children are not full of self-pride or arrogance, exalting themselves above others.

~~~~~~~

So, what can we conclude from these scriptures? God honors those who are humble; He hates a proud and arrogant spirit. But He does not want a false humility. He wants us to recognize that compared to His Son, we are but filthy rags. Desperately in need of a Savior. That goes for everybody, from the most powerful man on earth to the Gladys Finklesteins who clean the restrooms at your kid's elementary school. In God's eyes, the playing field is level. I won't be surprised, though, if Gladys has a front row seat waiting for her at the banquet in heaven!

REFLECTION TIME

Take a few moments to ponder the scriptures about humility. Are there people in your life that you tend to give greater importance to due to their position or power? How do these passages change your perspective?

_____

_____

_____

_____

_____

_____

_____

Search your heart and see if there are areas where you need to let go of a haughty or proud attitude. How can you change that to a genuinely humble attitude?

_____

_____

_____

_____

_____

_____

_____

Write out a prayer asking God to reveal the attitude of your heart, and to help you adapt a humble spirit that is demonstrated by Jesus.

_____

_____

_____

_____

_____

_____

Thank you, Lord, that you have given us clear direction about what You want the attitudes of our hearts to be. Thank you that you esteem the lowliest person, at least in man's eyes, to be higher than the most influential person we can think of in this world. Thank you for the example of Your Son who left His place on High to walk among us filthy sinners. And that You will lift us up into heaven to be with You. What an awesome thought! In Your name, Amen!

~~ ADDITIONAL NOTES ~~

~~DAY 12 ~~

A RELIGIOUS SMORGASBORD
(Jesus Is the Way)

In the United States alone, there are hundreds of religions. All are touting their belief systems (or non-beliefs, I guess, for the atheist folks!). Like the samples offered at the grocery store, you can try every single one until you find one that suits your tastes. But it can be very confusing. Even within denominations, there seem to be differing beliefs. There is actually "conservative" Christianity and "liberal" Christianity. Last time I checked, conservative and liberal viewpoints rarely find common ground.

You can worship anyone or anything you want — Jesus, Satan, Allah, Buddha, Mother Earth, saints, the sun, manmade idols. Every major religion has its own beliefs about the afterlife, salvation, how one gets to heaven, who Jesus is, even whether you should have musical instruments in the church. Churches have divided over some of the most non-religious issues you can imagine. And if this church's teaching isn't to your liking, you can move on down the road and try another one.

Despite all these differences, there seems to be a common belief that it truly doesn't matter what you believe; all roads lead to heaven. We should agree to accept and respect our differences. "COEXIST" and "TOLERANCE" were the bumper stickers of the day. Each letter was in the shape of a different religious symbol. "Can't we all just get along?" is the implication.

Well, the answer to those was another bumper sticker that said "CONTRADICT". Meaning they can't all be right. Which is true, since they all have different viewpoints of salvation.

So, let's dive into the scriptures and see what God, who made heaven and earth, has to say about it all.

FIRST WE MUST BELIEVE

"And as Moses lifted up the serpent in the wilderness, even so, must the Son of Man be lifted up, that whoever believes in Him should not perish but have eternal life. For God so loved the world that He gave His only begotten Son, that whoever believes in Him should not perish but have everlasting life. For God did not send His Son into the world to condemn the world, but that the world through Him might be saved." (John 3:14-17) Can you imagine being loved so much that someone would die in your place? That's exactly what Jesus did.

"And he brought them out and said, 'Sirs, what must I do to be saved?' So, they said, 'Believe on the Lord Jesus Christ, and you will be saved...'" (Acts 16:30-31) There must be a belief in the Son Jesus.

"Jesus declared, 'I am the resurrection and the life. He who believes in Me will live, even though he dies; and whoever lives and believes in Me will never die.'" (John 11:25-26). Even though we die a physical death, we will never die spiritually if we put our faith in Jesus Christ.

THERE IS ONLY ONE WAY

"Enter by the narrow gate; for wide is the gate and broad is the way that leads to destruction, and there are many who go in by it. Because narrow is the gate and difficult is the way which leads to life, and there are few who find it." (Matthew 7:13-14) Sadly, so many people are trying to find the easy way into heaven. The road is narrow, and it can be a difficult one at times. But, oh so rewarding!

"Jesus answered and said to him, 'Most assuredly, I say to you unless one is born again, he cannot see the kingdom of God.'" (John 3:3) We

MUST receive Jesus as our Lord and Savior if we want to spend eternity in heaven.

AND THAT WAY IS JESUS

"Let it be known to you all, and to all the people of Israel, that by the name of Jesus Christ of Nazareth, whom you crucified, whom God raised from the dead, by Him this man stands here before you whole. This is the 'stone, which was rejected by you builders, which has become the chief cornerstone.' Nor is there salvation in any other, for there is no other name under heaven given among men by which we must be saved." (Acts 4:10-12) No other person, thing, or belief will save us other than the saving knowledge of Jesus Christ.

"Jesus said to him, 'I am the way, the truth, and the life. No one comes to the Father except through Me.'" (John 14:6) Jesus is the gateway to the Father.

"For this is good and acceptable in the sight of God our Savior, who desires all men to be saved and to come to the knowledge of the truth. For there is one God and one Mediator between God and men, the Man Christ Jesus, who gave Himself a ransom for all, to be testified in due time." (1 Timothy 2:3-6) Jesus is the only way. Period.

~~~~~~~

Tying all these scriptures together, it is obvious there is only one way to heaven and eternal life with Jesus. The expression, "all roads lead to heaven" actually could be said to be true. Because one day we will ALL stand before Jesus. But only one belief is going to get you through those pearly gates. A saving belief in Jesus Christ as your Lord and Savior. Hallelujah!

REFLECTION TIME

Think about the things you have been taught about religion over the years. How do they fit with the scriptures we studied?

_____
_____
_____
_____
_____
_____
_____

Which scripture speaks to your heart, and why?

_____
_____
_____
_____
_____
_____
_____

Write a prayer, thanking Jesus for His free gift of salvation. If you do not have a relationship with Him, take a few moments and ask Him into your heart. Let that be your prayer.

_____
_____
_____
_____
_____
_____
_____

Thank You, Jesus, that you loved us so much that You gave Your life for us. Thank you that we don't have to look anywhere else but in Your Word to know the truth. As Peter said to You, **"Lord, to whom shall we go? You have the words of eternal life. Also, we have come to believe and know that You are the Christ, the Son of the living God."** *(John 6:68-69) What profound and comforting words! What an awesome God You are! In Your name we pray, Amen.*

~~ ADDITIONAL NOTES ~~

~~ DAY 13 ~~

ARE YOU PREPARED?

(Be Ready for His Coming)

Human nature is a curious thing. We plod along in our daily lives, just working out our agendas. Suddenly a big disaster hits somewhere. It might be an earthquake, tornado, flood, whatever. The evening news inundates us with "disaster preparedness" admonishments. Here come the survival kits. "Don't be caught off-guard when the next big one hits!" we are warned. But, as the sensation dies down, we return to the "in other news" mode and settle back down into that everyday routine.

I grew up in Southern California where we had our share of earthquakes. Every time one occurred, talk about the "big one" would inevitably come up. You know, the one that was supposed to break part of California off into the ocean. It hasn't happened yet. But very likely, somewhere along the west coast, there will be a huge one. And millions, who ignored the warnings, will be stuck with no more than a day's worth of rations. As an FYI, I have seen survival kits for sale that will provide a family of four with enough food for four days. And get this-it has a shelf life of 30 years!! I don't mean to be critical, but I must wonder what kind of Frankenfood I would be eating that can outlive me! "Are you prepared?" is the battle cry. Or, we take on the role of the Monday morning quarterback. You know, the barrage of who's to blame, how should we have handled things differently, what legislation needs to be passed to avoid this in the future. All this may be useful for moving forward, but not very helpful in the crisis.

So, what happens when we don't prepare for (fill in the blank)? At the least, we are inconvenienced. At most, our very lives may depend on surviving or not. We live in a highly apathetic society. If it doesn't impact me, it doesn't concern me. Or, maybe we have heard the doomsayers crying out so much that we get numb to it and we fall back into our apathetic mindset. Until we are shaken up again.

~~~~~

The Bible speaks a lot about the future. One-third of it is prophecy. There is a great deal of warning of what is to come for those who are not prepared. That is, in a right relationship with Jesus. Let's take a snapshot look at the parable of the ten wise and foolish virgins, as told in Matthew 25:1-13.

"Then the kingdom of heaven shall be likened to ten virgins who took their lamps and went out to meet the bridegroom. Now five of them were wise, and five were foolish. Those who were foolish took their lamps and took no oil with them, but the wise took oil in their vessels with their lamps. But while the bridegroom was delayed, they all slumbered and slept."

Here's a synopsis. The Bridegroom is Jesus. The five wise virgins represent those who are prepared and waiting expectantly for His coming. The foolish ones are not ready. They are caught off-guard when He returns. They may be "playing" Christian but are preoccupied with the things of this world. They are living in a mindset of apathy. Just like the folks who know that one day a big catastrophe will happen, yet they choose to do nothing to prepare for it. So, when the time comes, they look to the wise ones to bail them out of the jam.

~~~~~

Spiritual apathy comes with a price tag. Anywhere from missing out on the blessings that Jesus wants to give us, to the genuine danger of our eternal destiny. Since tomorrow is promised to no one, wouldn't it be wise to get things together right now, today? What would you rather hear from Jesus-

"His lord said to him, 'Well done, good and faithful servant; you were faithful over a few things, I will make you ruler over many things. Enter into the joy of your Lord.'" (Matthew 25:21)

Or this~

"Not everyone who says to Me, 'Lord, Lord,' shall enter the kingdom of heaven, but he who does the will of My Father in heaven. Many will say to Me in that day, 'Lord, Lord, have we not prophesied in Your name, cast out demons in Your name, and done many wonders in Your name?' And then I will declare to them, 'I never knew you; depart from Me, you who practice lawlessness!'" (Matthew 7:21-23).

I don't know about you, but I want to be able to say, at the end of my life, the same words that Paul the apostle said:

"I have fought the good fight, I have finished the race, I have kept the faith. Finally, there is laid up for me the crown of righteousness, which the Lord, the righteous Judge, will give to me on that Day, and not to me only but also to all who have loved His appearing." (2 Timothy 4:7-8)

Are you ready for the return of Jesus? If He were to call you home today, would you be able to say the words of Paul? Or would you be that foolish virgin who is caught off guard and not prepared to meet your Savior?

REFLECTION TIME

Take a few moments and examine your spiritual attitude. Is there an area where you used to be passionate about, but now it has grown a bit lukewarm, or even cold? Discuss below.

_____

_____

_____

_____

_____

_____

What changes can you make to be on fire again in those areas?

_____

_____

_____

_____

_____

_____

Write out a prayer asking God to stir up your heart again and create a stronger desire for His return.

_____

_____

_____

_____

_____

_____

Thank you, Jesus, that Your Word teaches us how to be ready for Your coming. We don't want to be caught unprepared. Help us to daily seek You and Your ways and be diligent in obeying Your Word. Thank You for Your love, mercy, and grace. In Your Strong name, Amen!

BENJAMIN BUTTON

(Relying on Our Own Strength)

My family and I are on a western TV show kick. There's a television station that plays nearly every western series ever made. We latched onto Wagon Train. This group of men leads families out west to start a new life. Their end destination is California during the gold rush era. Dreams of starting over and leaving the past behind loom large in the hearts of those whose lives have been torn apart by the Civil War. There's Major Adams the leader, Charley the cook, and Bill, the steady right-hand man. Then there's the scout master, Flint McCullough, the dashing cowboy, who can take on an entire tribe of attacking Indians with one hand tied behind his back. He's the one all the girls swoon over. I admit I have drooled a little myself....

I bring up Flint because he is relevant to this illustration. In a recent episode, an elderly man, who I will call "Benjamin", went with Flint and his future grandson-in-law, whom I will dub "Luke", to find a source of water for the wagon train. While up in the mountain area, Benjamin lost his footing and fell to the ground below, seriously injuring himself. Due to the extent of his injuries, he could not be safely moved, so Flint and Luke could not return to the wagon train. In the meantime, Flint got bit by a rattle snake and became delirious. The danger was high due to impending Indian attacks. Despite his grave injuries, Benjamin kept hanging on, preventing the men from fleeing to safety. In desperation (now dealing with two incapacitated men) Luke decided to hasten Benjamin's death and smothered the man with Flint's jacket. In the struggle, Ben managed to grab a button off of the jacket. Thinking Ben was dead, Luke buried him in a shallow grave. He then packed up Flint and fled to catch up to the wagon train.

Meanwhile, back at the burial site, we see the earth move, and suddenly a hand thrusts up through the dirt with a button clinched tightly in the fist. BENJAMIN'S ALIVE! This button became his motivation to survive, and he dragged himself through the desert, and somehow through sheer determination, he caught up with the wagon train. (The train had stopped to search for water.) Flint, seeing it was his button and having been delirious at the time of Ben's "death", was afraid that he was the one who had tried to kill Benjamin. But the truth came out, and the old man eventually forgave Luke, and they all lived happily ever after.

~~~~~~~

Whew! Only in Hollywood, right? So why did I describe all that? To show how sheer will power and determination can see us through the darkest valley? Nooo… in the TV show, the button was Ben's emotional lifeline, the thing that kept him going in the face of an enormous situation.

My point here is to show a contrast to real life. Let's put God in that illustration. We are the old man who is facing a seemingly impossible situation. But unlike grandpa, we don't have to rely on our own strength to see us through. On the contrary, think of God as the button. He tells us to do the exact opposite.

RELY ON GOD'S STRENGTH

"In my distress, I called upon the Lord, and cried out to my God; He heard my voice from His temple, and my cry came before Him, even to His ears." (Psalm 18:6). God will hear my desperate cry for help all the way from heaven! And the cries of His children will not fall on deaf ears.

"I can do all things through Christ who strengthens me." (Philippians 4:13) We can try to do things in our own power, but we are limited. With Christ, we can do ALL things.

69

"...God resists the proud but gives grace to the humble. Therefore humble yourselves under the mighty hand of God, that He may exalt you in due time, casting all your care upon Him, for He cares for you." (1 Peter 5:5-7). It's interesting how our pride and "self-dependence" get in the way of seeking help for a problem. Not only does God want us to seek Him, but He wants us to give the problem entirely over to Him.

"The Lord is my strength and my shield; my heart trusted in Him, and I am helped. Therefore my heart greatly rejoices, and with my song, I will praise Him." (Psalm 28:7) If we trust in the Lord to be there when we call on Him-and we can-we should sing songs of praise to His name!

"And He said to me, 'My grace is sufficient for you, for My strength is made perfect in weakness.' Therefore most gladly I will rather boast in my infirmities, that the power of Christ may rest upon me." (2 Corinthians 12:9) When we are at our weakest, God will show Himself strong in us.

~~~~~~~

So we have 2 distinct scenarios here. We have grandpa doing things in his own strength, through his own determination. On the other hand, when we seek Jesus, we will have all the strength that we need, with Him leading the way. I don't know about you, but I think I would rather have God be my strength, which is unlimited. Then I can do more than I could ever imagine than if left to my own devices. I think the choice is pretty clear! We just need to let go of the pride of self-dependence and become totally dependent on Him. *"Pride goes before destruction, and a haughty spirit before a fall."* (Proverbs 16:18)

~~~~~~~

REFLECTION TIME

Think of a time when you were faced with a challenge and tried to do it in your own strength. Describe the difficulty you faced going it alone.

_____

_____

_____

_____

_____

_____

What difference would it have made had you turned it over to the Lord, and let Him take care of things?

_____

_____

_____

_____

_____

_____

Write a prayer asking God to remind you of His strength and thanking Him for being there when you call.

_____

_____

_____

_____

_____

_____

_____

Thank You, Lord Jesus for Your promise that You will always be with us, giving us the strength we need in any trial. Forgive us when we try to do things on our own. Keep us always mindful of Your presence. In Your name, Amen!

~~ DAY 15 ~~

DIRTY SNOW

(The Stain of Sin)

There's nothing more beautiful than a fresh layer of snow. Pristine, untouched, pure.

In the Pacific Northwest, we had an unusual amount of snow this winter. Seattle had their highest total on record, and up north, about an hour away, we had eight inches. Now, before you Midwesterners start to snicker, please remember that we are known and equipped for rain, not snow! Snowplows are a scarce commodity here. Another problem we have to contend with is the hills. We have some streets that would rival San Francisco! Couple that with snow and ice, and you have a recipe for disaster.

When snow first falls, you have a sense of purity, serenity, peace. Untouched by humans, it is breathtaking. But it doesn't last forever. (This is a rural area, so there are a lot of dirt and gravel roads.) The snow gradually loses its purity and becomes slushy, brown, and muddy. Just a big mess. I like to call it "Dirty Snow". Hey, that would have made a cool name for a grunge band, which incidentally, emerged in the '80s in Seattle! (Alternative rock-not exactly my cup of tea!)

Sin is a lot like that dirty snow. It corrupts what God has made beautiful. It permeates our hearts, and mingles with our thoughts, making everything it touches ugly.

That was not God's intention. He created the most beautiful, perfect place called the Garden of Eden. He created man and put him in charge of it. You know the story. Adam and Eve messed it up like humans

72

always seem to do. Sin was born, and we have been dealing with it ever since.

But God, in His infinite grace and mercy, made a way to free us of the sin that would eternally separate us from Him. He sent His son, the Lamb of God, to pay the penalty for us. Let's look at some scriptures:

THE REPUCUSSIONS OF SIN

"For the wages of sin is death, but the gift of God is eternal life in Christ Jesus our Lord." (Romans 6:23). The ultimate price of unrepentant sin is death and eternal separation from God.

"As drought and heat consume the snow waters, so the grave consumes those who have sinned." (Job 24:19) Winter snow is melted by the heat and dryness of the changing weather. It will eventually dry up or soak into the ground. Sin takes us to a watery grave if we don't seek repentance.

"The destruction of transgressors and sinners shall be together, and those who forsake the Lord shall be consumed." (Isaiah 1:28) Without Jesus, we have no hope for forgiveness and healing.

BUT JESUS MADE A WAY

"Come now, and let us reason together," Says the Lord, *"Though your sins are like scarlet, they shall be as white as snow; though they are red like crimson, they shall be as wool."* (Isaiah 1:18) Isn't it interesting that our sins are like scarlet, and they are washed white by blood, which is red. But this is the pure, sinless blood of Jesus Christ.

"In Him, we have redemption through His blood, the forgiveness of sins, according to the riches of His grace." (Ephesians 1:7) Grace. We don't deserve it. But Jesus loves us so much, that He freely bestows it upon us.

"If we confess our sins, He is faithful and just to forgive us our sins and to cleanse us from all unrighteousness." (1 John 1:9) Jesus can

make us pure and as white as snow, but first, we have to confess and ask for forgiveness. It is there, just for the asking.

"And behold, a leper came and worshiped Him, saying, "Lord, if You are willing, You can make me clean."" (Matthew 8:2) Lepers in Biblical times were considered unclean, and full of sin. It was an incurable disease, but Jesus, with just a touch, could heal the person just as He can cleanse us from all sin.

"Purge me with hyssop, and I shall be clean; wash me, and I shall be whiter than snow." (Psalm 51:7) Hyssop was used for purification purposes, and also as an antiseptic. It was a healing and cleansing agent used in Old Testament times. Now we have the cleansing power of Jesus Christ through the shedding of His blood.

I believe it is clear from these scriptures that snow represents a clean heart. We are stained with the crimson blood of sin. But we have a Savior who shed His blood to heal us, cleanse us and save us from eternal damnation. That is so awesome!!!!

~~~~~~~

So the winter has come and gone. The snow, which fell pure and clean, was eventually dirtied by the comings and goings of the residents here. Huge ugly mounds piled up where the plows dumped the snow while clearing roads. But Spring has started to wake out of its slumber, and new life is forming everywhere. And the snow has melted. There is a time of renewal and refreshing. Fortunately for us, we don't have to wait for the seasons to change. All we need to do is cry out to Jesus, ask to be forgiven, washed and purified. His blood has covered all of humanity, past present and future. What an amazing gift He gave us!

74

REFLECTION TIME

Take a moment and ponder the scriptures we have studied. How do you connect Biblical snow to Jesus?

_____
_____
_____
_____
_____
_____
_____

What areas in your heart need to be washed clean and made pure? List them below:

_____
_____
_____
_____
_____
_____
_____

Ask Jesus to forgive you for these sins and to wash you clean!

_____
_____
_____
_____
_____
_____
_____

Dear Jesus: Thank you for the cleansing power of Your blood that You shed at Calvary. Thank you that all I need to do is come to you in repentance and with a contrite heart. You will wash me clean, pure as snow. Forgiven and restored. How amazing is Your grace! In Your name, AMEN!

∼ ADDITONAL NOTES ∼

THE COST OF SIN

(It Comes with a Price Tag!)

When I was in grade school, my best friend, Sally, lived across the street. (The names have been changed to protect the guilty!) We hung out together almost daily. One of the things we liked to do was play catch in her front yard. Another thing we liked to do was visit her neighbor's garden. Next door to her was a huge house that was owned by the local Catholic school. It housed the priests that taught at the high school. One of the priests, Father Higley had a beautiful garden. During the summer, we would go over and visit, and he would let us eat some of the ripened fruit. One delectable bounty was his boysenberry patch. So scrumptious!

Sally and I were, for the most part, pretty well behaved. We kept ourselves out of trouble. Except for one thing. The temptation of the berries was just too much for us. So we would play catch in her front yard and deliberately throw the ball over the fence so it would land in the boysenberries. Of course we had to go get the ball, so we would slip in through the side gate and sneak into the patch and munch on the berries. One time, Father Higley caught us in the act. With a twinkle in his eye, he asked us if we had been eating them. "No!" we firmly replied. But I have a feeling the stains on our hands and faces told a different story! He let us get away with it and back home we went.

Sin has a way of finding you out. At least that's what I thought in this case. Shortly after our escapade, Sally and I were playing ball in her backyard. We had kicked off our shoes and were running around barefoot. Sally threw the ball and it landed in the flower bed. I ran in after it, not knowing that the flower bed had a huge cactus tree with needle-like quills which had dropped on the ground. That's right, my poor little feet looked like pin cushions! As Sally's grandpa was gingerly pulling them out of my feet, I sat there, convinced this was payback for the berry theft! I just knew that I was doing penance and I wasn't even Catholic! I don't think we visited the berry patch again....

~~~~~~~

THE CONSEQUENCES OF SIN

"If you do well, will you not be accepted? And if you do not do well, sin lies at the door. And its desire is for you, but you should rule over it." (Genesis 4:7) Sin is like a stray cat scratching at your door. So cute and helpless looking, it draws you in. But watch out! If you feed it, it will always be knocking at the door!

"Let no one say when he is tempted, 'I am tempted by God'; for God cannot be tempted by evil, nor does He Himself tempt anyone. But each one is tempted when he is drawn away by his own desires and enticed. Then, when desire has conceived, it gives birth to sin; and sin, when it is full-grown, brings forth death." (James 1:13-15) Sin is like quicksand. As soon as you give in to the desire, you will be drawn in further and further. But we need to understand where the temptation comes from. It doesn't come from God, but from the enemy. The good news is that God will provide a way out.

"For I know that in me (that is, in my flesh) nothing good dwells; for to will is present with me, but how to perform what is good I do not find. For the good that I will to do, I do not do; but the evil I will not to do, that I practice. Now if I do what I will not to do, it is no longer I who do it, but sin that dwells in me." (Romans 7:18-20) Ah, that endless battle between good and evil; the constant struggle of the flesh and the Spirit. We have the desire to do good, but often lack the determination. But evil seems to come so easily.

"Do not be deceived, God is not mocked; for whatever a man sows, that he will also reap. For he who sows to his flesh will of the flesh reap corruption, but he who sows to the Spirit will of the Spirit reap

everlasting life." (Galatians 6:7-8). There are consequences for our sin. There is also forgiveness because of the cross.

"...you have sinned against the Lord; and be sure your sin will find you out." (Numbers 32:23) We cannot hide anything from God. And ultimately, all sin is a sin against Him.

FORGIVENESS OF SIN

"If we confess our sins, He is faithful and just to forgive us our sins and to cleanse us from all unrighteousness." (1 John 1:9) What a comforting thought. Although we are forgiven when we truly repent, our desire should be to turn away from the sin and get back to that close walk with Jesus.

"In Him we have redemption through His blood, the forgiveness of sins, according to the riches of His grace." (Ephesians 1:7) What an immense price Jesus paid so we wouldn't have to owe the debt. May we never lose sight of the enormity of His act.

"For this is My blood of the new covenant, which is shed for many for the remission of sins." (Matthew 26:28) During the Last Supper, Jesus was describing the representation of His blood that would be poured out on the cross, which would allow for the atonement of our sins.

~~~~~~~

Getting back to Sally and me. We did something wrong and we got busted. It stopped the behavior. But I wonder if it changed our hearts. We knew we shouldn't have done that, yet we did it anyway. Now there are a lot worse things we could have done other than snitch a few berries. But in the eyes of the Lord, wrong is wrong. Whether the needles were retribution for my sin, only God knows. The juice stains washed away with soap and water. But the stain of sin required the washing through the blood of Jesus. And He provided that on the cross. How precious that gift is!

79

REFLECTION TIME

Think back to a time when you knowingly engaged in sin. What was the cost?

_____

_____

_____

_____

_____

_____

_____

How do you deal with the constant battle between the flesh and the Spirit?

_____

_____

_____

_____

_____

_____

Write out a prayer thanking God for that precious gift of forgiveness and ask Him to help you resist the wiles of the enemy.

_____

_____

_____

_____

_____

_____

Thank you, Lord Jesus, for the penalty You paid for our sins. We have feet of clay and will always be battling the war of the flesh vs. Spirit. Help us to walk closely with You, so that the enemy cannot get a foothold in our lives. In Your name, Amen!

~~ ADDITIONAL NOTES ~~

NOW, WHERE WAS I...
(Distraction)

Distraction; the writer's enemy. I can't tell you how many times I have sat down to write, only to have fifty interruptions! Just this morning, the house is quiet, the animals are both sleeping. Until I settle down, that is. Suddenly, the dog needs to go outside to do his business. The cat wakes up and has to nose around my computer. Oh, now the neighbor decides to mow his lawn. And soon it will be lunchtime....

I have found distraction to be a typical pattern in my life. This intensifies when the pressure is on to get something done. I tend to be a procrastinator. If there are two weeks to get a project done, in my mind, it feels like three weeks. "Oh, I have lots of time" is the prevailing thought. I admit I seem to do my best work under pressure, but it certainly does add stress. And I am really in trouble if there is no deadline or someone whom to be accountable. Self-discipline is not my friend, which is why my new exercise machine has been sitting in the box for over a month now!

I get easily distracted by my surroundings as well. I remember when I was in school, studying outside, enjoying the sunshine and fresh air seemed like a great idea. But the scenery around me lulled my mind away from my academics. I didn't accomplish very much. I think I need to hole myself up in a small room with no windows!

Satan is well aware of the tool of distraction. He has used it on me many times, with great success. He knows that if he can get my mind off of Jesus and onto the situation at hand, I am temporarily separated from God. Oh, he knows that he can't take me down completely. My love for Jesus is too strong. But if he can put a wedge in there somewhere, he has gained a momentary victory.

I have another bad habit. Starting things and not finishing them. I have a bookcase full of partially read books, unfinished bible studies, and a craft room with supplies for a myriad of new projects I wanted to do. It's shameful. It is safe to say I am not a good steward of my time. New year's resolutions are wasted on me. Usually, they never leave the page on which they are written.

~~~~~~~

The Bible talks about keeping our eyes on the prize. We have a purpose beyond this earthly existence.

KEEP YOUR EYES ON THE PRIZE!

"I press toward the goal for the prize of the upward call of God in Christ Jesus." (Philippians 3:14) The apostle Paul exhorts us to keep our eye on what God is calling us to. Not my own agenda, not what the world is telling me to do. But what God is calling me to.

"Therefore we also, since we are surrounded by so great a cloud of witnesses, let us lay aside every weight, and the sin which so easily ensnares us, and let us run with endurance the race that is set before us, looking unto Jesus, the author and finisher of our faith, who for the joy that was set before Him endured the cross, despising the shame, and has sat down at the right hand of the throne of God." (Hebrews 12:1-2) Don't let the distractions of the world, and all its enticement get us off course in our race. Let Jesus be our example.

"And He is the head of the body, the church, who is the beginning, the firstborn from the dead, that in all things He may have the preeminence." (Colossians 1:18) We need to consciously remember that Jesus needs to be #1 in our hearts and lives.

HOW DO WE STAY FOCUSED?

"If then you were raised with Christ, seek those things which are above, where Christ is, sitting at the right hand of God. Set your mind on things above, not on things on the earth. For you died, and your life is hidden with Christ in God. When Christ who is our life appears, then

you also will appear with Him in glory." (Colossians 3:1-4) Our focus needs to be on Christ and heavenly things, rather than the temporal things of earth. We have a heavenly calling. Can you imagine what it will be like in heaven with Him? Greater than anything we could think!

"Your ears shall hear a word behind you, saying, 'This is the way, walk in it' whenever you turn to the right hand or whenever you turn to the left." (Isaiah 30:21) When we are distracted, we cannot hear the voice of God directing us. We need to be focused on Him. Otherwise, that voice might be the enemy's.

"You will keep him in perfect peace, whose mind is stayed on You because he trusts in You." (Isaiah 26:3) Another good reason to stay focused on Jesus! Beautiful, sweet peace.

"Let your eyes look straight ahead, and your eyelids look right before you." (Proverbs 4:25). Keep Jesus straight in front of you, and then you cannot be distracted by the enemy.

~~~~~~

So God wants our eyes on Him and doing His will. Satan wants to do everything he can to disrupt that. I need to be able to recognize when this happens so that I can refocus on the tasks that God has put before me. If I am purposing in my heart to put God first before all things, I will have much greater success and a deeper peace about what I am doing. I will gladly take that in this crazy world! (I think I hear my stomach growling…. must be time for lunch!)

REFLECTION TIME

How does Satan go about distracting you in your walk with Jesus?

_____

_____

_____

_____

_____

_____

_____

What are some tools you can use to keep Satan at bay?

_____

_____

_____

_____

_____

_____

_____

Write out a prayer, asking God to help you stay focused and on Him.

_____

_____

_____

_____

_____

_____

_____

Thank you, Jesus, that you love us and that you have a special calling on each of our lives. Help us to commit to putting You first. Thank You that You have provided everything we need in Your Word. Help us to be diligent in digging into it every single day. In Your name, Amen!

~~ ADDITIONAL NOTES ~~

~~ DAY 18 ~~

TRYING TO FIND THE PERFECT RECIPE

(Seeking the Truth)

Have you ever experienced wanting to create a beautiful, thriving garden using the right seeds, soil, adequate sunlight, water etc. and no matter how much you do right, something goes wrong? You plant your seeds, and they sprout. For a while, everything's looking wonderful, until one day you notice the leaves on your spinach are looking a bit pale. Jaundiced might be a better description. So, you start researching the cause. Your confusion is just beginning as you learn it could be too much water, too little water, too much sun, too much shade, too much potassium, not enough niacin. Wowsa! Seems the more you ask, the more varied the advice. So what do you do? Do you keep researching the problem, hoping that someone knows what they are talking about? I guess, try one thing, then if that doesn't work, try the opposite. Meanwhile, your little spinach plants are about to bite the dust.

Or how about cooking? Have you ever been faced with the same dilemma on how to save your kitchen disaster? Checking your recipe to find out what went wrong, only to read conflicting information? Here's a story for you. Many years ago, I decided to make a cherry pie for my dad's birthday, as it was his favorite pie. I followed the recipe to the letter. Everything was going beautifully until it came time to roll the dough out. For the life of me, I couldn't get the mixture to stay together! In my frustration, I called my mom, an expert pie maker. She said it might need more shortening, or more water, maybe too much flour. Thanks, Mom! That sounded just like the gardening advice I got about my spinach. NOT helpful! I was so frustrated I was to the point of tears.

Unfortunately, my sister chose to walk in the door at that moment. Before she could even say hello, I bellowed at her, "DON'T SAY A WORD TO ME RIGHT NOW!!!" Sizing up the situation very quickly, she beat a hasty retreat to the living room! I wanted to throw the ball of dough clear across the room. It probably would have disintegrated on impact! Or it might have hit my sister in the back as she was ducking for cover.

Instead, I decided to go straight to the pie queen herself. I packed up my lump of dough and headed over to Mom's house. I walked in the door, ceremoniously handed her the bowl and said, "Here! Fix this!" She took the pie dough out of my hands, checked the texture, weaved her magic, and voila! The perfect pie crust. (I never did find out what she did to fix it. Maybe she simply added her own special love!) It's interesting to me that the pie crust recipe originally came from her. Did she secretly leave something out? Nah, she wouldn't do that. But the thought DID cross my mind....

~~~~~~~

Life is full of lumpy dough, yellow leaves, and a constant barrage of problems. So many times, we look under every rock for the answer to the problem. The so-called "experts" will often be more confusion than help. Sometimes, if we are honest, we will ask everyone in sight until we get the answer we want to hear, validating our position. Unfortunately, people's viewpoints are often skewed by their personal experience. Not necessarily based on fact, and it may not be reliable.

There is one thing, though, that we can always count on to be true. God is never-changing, always constant. His Word is the same yesterday, today and tomorrow. What applied 4,000 years ago is still valid today. You don't have to worry about the latest research turning His Word inside out. (Actually, man has been trying to do that with every false religion since Biblical times. But that's a discussion for another day!) The ten commandments that were given to Moses still apply, right? Murder, covetousness, idolatry, theft. They are still wrong. Check out these scriptures:

HIS WORD IS UNCHANGING

"Heaven and earth will pass away, but My words will by no means pass away." (Mark 13:31) God's Word stands the test of time. No amount of scientific research can disprove it.

"Jesus Christ is the same yesterday, today, and forever. Do not be carried about with various and strange doctrines." (Hebrews 13:8-9) Man is always trying to twist the Word of God and cast doubt on who Jesus is. But that is impossible. He is immutable. His words endure forever. But there is a warning here. We cannot let false teachers sway us from the truth. Always measure everything against scripture.

"The grass withers, the flower fades, but the word of our God stands forever." (Isaiah 40:8) Everything around us is dying, but God's Word will last through eternity.

WHAT ARE WE TO DO?

"Therefore you shall lay up these words of Mine in your heart and in your soul, and bind them as a sign on your hand, and they shall be as frontlets between your eyes." (Deuteronomy 11:18) We need to study God's Word, hide these precious passages in our hearts, so that we will remember them. In Judaism, a frontlet is passages of scripture written on pieces of paper and attached by a band, and then worn around the forehead.

"And it shall be with him, and he shall read it all the days of his life, that he may learn to fear the Lord his God and be careful to observe all the words of this law and these statutes." (Deuteronomy 17:19) We need to read, study, and apply God's Word to our lives. We cannot go astray if we do this on a regular basis.

"Remember His covenant forever, the Word which He commanded, for a thousand generations." (1 Chronicles 16:15) God's promises and commandments are as relative to us as they were in the days of Moses.

It is so reassuring to know that we can rely on God's Word, no matter how the world tries to corrupt it. And if you find your "dough" lumpy and dry, seek Him out. After all, He is the Provider of our daily bread. Not even the best chef in the world can compete with the Master!

REFLECTION TIME

How do these scriptures give you confidence in His Word?

_____

_____

_____

_____

_____

_____

Describe how trusting the endurance of God's Word has helped guide you.

_____

_____

_____

_____

_____

_____

Write a prayer asking God to help you discern His Word over the advice of man.

_____

_____

_____

_____

_____

_____

Thank you, Lord Jesus, that Your Word has stood the test of time. Thank you that we can trust the power of it, and that it is unchanging. Help us to resist the temptation to look to man for answers before we seek Your face. Everything we need to know can be found in the pages of Your book. What a gift that is! In Your precious name, Amen!.

~~ DAY 19 ~~

EARTHLY POSSESSIONS VS. HEAVENLY TREASURES

(Which One Do You Want?)

I'm sure you have heard the saying, "He who dies with the most toys wins." It was made into a bumper sticker. An expression a lot of people seem to have taken to heart.

Some people are driven to collect as much wealth, possessions and power as they possibly can. They scratch and claw their way up the corporate ladder to get that corner office. Sometimes they don't care who they step on getting to the top. They will sacrifice family, friends or health to grasp that brass ring.

Fame and fortune are a fantasy for most people. They only dream about it. They see the high-powered CEOs with their cars, private jet, endless bank account and think, "Wow, I wish I could have that. Then all my troubles would be gone." Celebrities seem to have it all. Riches beyond their wildest dreams, adoring fans, global notoriety, an entourage to wait on them hand and foot. It all looks pretty amazing.

But looks can be deceiving. The fact of the matter is that celebrities seem to be the most miserable of all. Yes, they have all the material possessions they want, but if you listen to the interviews, there are countless admissions of emptiness and loneliness. Drug use is rampant in the entertainment world. They seem to lose their identity in all the notoriety and find themselves craving a sense of normalcy.

On the other side of the coin is the expression "You never see a hearse pulling a U-Haul!" What does this mean? You can't take it with you. There was a counterpoint made regarding the toys. "The one with the most toys still dies." Both sayings are accurate, and point out that possessions are just that-possessions. Stuff.

Trying to "have it all" can be a vicious cycle. We work 80 hours a week so we can buy our dream home and all our toys. But because we are working so much, we don't have time to enjoy these toys we are working so hard for in the first place! That doesn't make a whole lot of sense.

We are always looking for that one thing that will satisfy. Whether it's the latest high-tech gadget, the upgraded software, or the newest I-phone. But it never seems to end. There will always be an upgrade or new model. Bigger, faster, cooler, younger. All appealing to the lust of our flesh. The "shiny new object syndrome"!

~~~~~~

But Jesus has a different perspective. He is everlasting. His rewards never tarnish, go out-of-date, or fail. They all have an eternal value that cannot be measured by earthly standards. We will be given heavenly crowns, rewarding our faithfulness.

WORLDLY POSSESSIONS DON'T SATISFY

"Do not lay up for yourselves treasures on earth, where moth and rust destroy and where thieves break in and steal; but lay up for yourselves treasures in heaven, where neither moth nor rust destroys and where thieves do not break in and steal. For where your treasure is, there your heart will be also." (Matthew 6:19-21) All manmade things have a shelf life. They deteriorate, get stolen or lost. But the treasures in heaven are far greater and will last through eternity.

"For what profit is it to a man if he gains the whole world, and loses his own soul? Or what will a man give in exchange for his soul? For

the Son of Man will come in the glory of His Father with His angels, and then He will reward each according to his works." (Matthew 16:26-27) It is far better to be rewarded for our works that glorify God,

93

then to sacrifice them on the altar of worldly ambitions.

GOD REWARDS TRUE "HEAVENLY" WORKS

"Finally, there is laid up for me the crown of righteousness, which the Lord, the righteous Judge, will give to me on that Day, and not to me only but also to all who have loved His appearing." (2 Timothy 4:8) There will be a reward for those who long for and live for His Second coming. Material possessions will pale in comparison to this great reward!

"And whatever you do, do it heartily, as to the Lord and not to men, knowing that from the Lord you will receive the reward of the inheritance; for you serve the Lord Christ." (Colossians 3:23-24). We are to conduct our lives to reflect our love for the Lord and not with the desire to please man. The inheritance we will receive as His servants outweigh any earthly accolades.

"For God is not unjust to forget your work and labor of love which you have shown toward His name, in that you have ministered to the saints, and do minister. And we desire that each one of you show the same diligence to the full assurance of hope until the end, that you do not become sluggish, but imitate those who through faith and patience inherit the promises." (Hebrews 6:10-12). God will remember all of our works and acts of love that are done in His name.

"And let us not grow weary while doing good, for in due season we shall reap if we do not lose heart." (Galatians 6:9) We need to keep pressing in when we get tired.

It is far better to keep our eye on the heavenly prize, rather than on the temporal things of this earth. But we also must not take the attitude of living for Jesus so that we get rewards in heaven or even blessings here on earth. It should come from a willing heart, as an expression of gratitude for the ultimate gift of everlasting life He gave us. We can never repay that in full!

REFLECTION TIME

Has there been a time in your life when you strove to obtain earthly possessions, or had your eye on that one shiny object? Did it satisfy your soul, or did it feel empty and dissatisfying?

_____

_____

_____

_____

_____

_____

_____

What kind of heavenly treasures can you "send up ahead"? How will you go about doing that?

_____

_____

_____

_____

_____

_____

_____

Write out a prayer asking God for direction, and for the desire to forsake earthly things that do not give us eternal satisfaction.

_____

_____

_____

_____

_____

_____

_____

Dear Father: Thank You that You have given us things to enjoy in this life here on earth. But like anything, we can get carried away, and let our possessions, desires, goals possess us. Help us to keep our eye on things above and to strive to store up those heavenly treasures which are safely kept in Your loving hands. In Your precious name, Amen!

~~ ADDITIONAL NOTES ~~

~ DAY 20 ~

DEPENDENCE DAY

(Self-Sufficiency)

*Stand on your own two feet
*Pull yourself up by your own bootstraps
*I am Woman, hear me roar! (An obnoxious song from the '70s)
*If it's to be, it's up to me
*I am my own man (or woman)
*Doing things by my strength

Back in the late sixties, a movement began, called "Women's Liberation" which was a call for political alignment of women and feminist intellectualism. "We are strong!" was the battle cry. We don't need men! We can do anything men can do. Equality for all! That is all well and good, and in Biblical times women were considered far beneath men. Sadly, there are still countries who oppress women. But this particular movement went beyond equality and virtually castrated men of their masculinity. That's my humble opinion, and I am sticking to it!

The bottom line is people have the mindset that they don't need anybody else. I am going to do what I want when I want and how I want. Nobody is going to tell me differently. "Resist authority" is the new mantra. What has happened here is that modern thinking has become self-centered, me-focused. A pastor joked once that the magazine titles have gone from "People" to "Us" to "You" to "Self". Just watch people around you when you are out and about. Or look at Facebook posts. The selfie has become a way of life. I was in a public restroom the other day, and I kid you not, a teenage girl was standing there in the middle of the bathroom taking selfies while waiting for her mom. Really?? (Sorry, I think I am digressing here!)

Being self-sufficient is fine up to a point. Until we decide we don't need each other. Once again, the world's view on things clashes with Biblical truth. While the world tells us that we are weak if we rely on others, God

tells us when we are weak, we are strong! Let me explain that apparent oxymoron:

God wants us to be totally and utterly dependent on Him. He does not want us to be relying on our self-sufficiency. We are to come to Him as little children with our needs, our desires, our fears, our hopes, our dreams. Because we are looking to Him to supply our strength, His power manifests itself in us, and that is infinitely stronger than our puny attempts.

The problem a lot of people have with this teaching is that it flies in the face of our independence. We want to do things our way. Maybe it's that need for control. It can be scary to let things go and let someone else take over. Self-reliance is an issue I have dealt with many times. I have had jobs where I worked independently, and other jobs where I have been a manager. The need to control the situation is there. Could it be that I don't trust the other person to carry on with what I have started? Or possibly am I afraid it won't be up to my standards? You know that attitude, "If you want something done right, you've got to do it yourself." Or it's just easier and faster to do it myself.

GOD'S PERSPECTIVE ON MY WEAKNESS

"And He said to me, 'My grace is sufficient for you, for My strength is made perfect in weakness.' Therefore most gladly I will rather boast in my infirmities, that the power of Christ may rest upon me." (2 Corinthians 12:9) He will provide whatever I need, especially when I am at my weakest.

"Now to Him who is able to do exceedingly abundantly above all that we ask or think, according to the power that works in us." (Ephesians 3:20). My thoughts are limited. His power is infinitely higher than mine.

"'Not by might nor by power, but by my Spirit', says the LORD of hosts." (Zechariah 4:6). Does this say by Debbie's might or power??

Nooooo… it says by His Spirit, which is far more potent than anything I could muster.

WHAT MY RESPONSE SHOULD BE

"Therefore I take pleasure in infirmities, in reproaches, in needs, in persecutions, in distresses, for Christ's sake. For when I am weak, then I am strong." (2 Corinthians 12:10) Because He will give me supernatural strength for the trial, I can rest easy no matter what the circumstance.

"Trust in the Lord with all your heart and lean not on your own understanding; In all your ways acknowledge Him, and He shall direct your paths." (Proverbs 3:5-6) Seek Him out first, and He will lead you through whatever is troubling you.

"But now indeed there are many members, yet one body. And the eye cannot say to the hand, 'I have no need of you'; nor again the head to the feet, 'I have no need of you.' No, much rather, those members of the body which seem to be weaker are necessary." (1 Corinthians 12:20-22). We need to remember that as Christians, we form a body, each needing to work together, and not independent of each other.

So after studying these passages, I know that I don't have to rely on my own strength. Not only do I not have to, but I am told NOT to. Jesus is there waiting to provide whatever I need, whenever I need it. Jesus instructs us to give everything over to Him. There is a sense of peace in knowing that there is Someone who knows better than I do, whom I can call on for guidance. I also need to remember that He sometimes provides what I need by placing people in my life to help me, and that I can be a help to as well. All of us working together to do the will of the Master. Time to let go of that pride!

REFLECTION TIME

Think of a situation where you relied on your own strength. How would things have been different if you had sought the Lord first?

_____
_____
_____
_____
_____
_____
_____

What does seeking the Lord look like to you?

_____
_____
_____
_____
_____
_____
_____

Write out a prayer asking God to manifest His strength and to give you the guidance you need in your particular situation.

_____
_____
_____
_____
_____
_____
_____

Dear Heavenly Father: Thank you that You have provided guidance and strength and that I don't have to rely on my own ways. Your plans and ways are much higher than mine; above anything I could ask or think. Thank you for your love, grace, and patience. Amen!

~~ ADDITIONAL NOTES ~~

IN THE LIGHT OF DAY

(Jesus Is the Light)

Have you ever noticed how much scarier things seem to be at night than in the daylight? Shadows loom the size of giants, noises are so much louder, and everything has a creepy feeling. Light seems to bring us comfort. I have to laugh because I can "hear" a sound better when the light is on. If something disturbs me in the middle of the night, I will sit up in bed. Turning on the light helps to make the boogie man go away.

But sometimes the light can reveal things we really don't want to see. Tornadoes, earthquakes, floods that happen in the dead of night can do a lot of damage. It's not until the morning comes when the real destruction is exposed. Devastation abounds. The harsh reality of day reveals a far greater truth than we feared.

No doubt, we all have "darkness" inside our hearts that we wouldn't want exposed to the light of day. Anger, bitterness, resentment, jealousy-these are all things that we try to hide amongst the shadows. If they were to be exposed, it wouldn't be pretty. And guess who is waiting for the perfect moment to pounce?

~~~~~~~~

We have an adversary, Satan, that lurks in the darkness. Like a snake, he slithers around in the recesses of our lives. He likes to do the most damage when we cannot see him. He moves like a stealth bomber, zeroing in on his unsuspecting target. Satan is a dirty player. He will lure you into something that you know you shouldn't do, and then when he

102

has you hooked, he will come along and condemn you for doing precisely that — exposing us in the light of day.

The Bible has many names for this enemy. "Satan" means adversary. He is also known as the tempter, the accuser, the destroyer, the murderer, ruler of this world, Beelzebub, and the devil, among others.

SATAN'S TACTICS

"For Satan himself transforms himself into an angel of light." (2 Corinthians 11:14). Satan will masquerade as light and goodness, where in reality he is purely evil, with evil intents.

"The thief does not come except to steal, and to kill, and to destroy..." (John 10:10). He has one purpose, and that is to destroy what God has created.

"...the accuser of our brethren, who accused them before our God day and night..." (Revelation 12:10) His accusations against us are relentless.

JESUS IS OUR ADVOCATE

"Therefore submit to God. Resist the devil, and he will flee from you." (James 4:7). The first step we need to take to avoid falling victim is to submit to our heavenly Father in humility. Listen to what He calls us to do. Then rely on His strength to turn away from the temptations of Satan.

"For it is the God who commanded light to shine out of darkness, who has shone in our hearts to give the light of the knowledge of the glory of God in the face of Jesus Christ." (2 Corinthians 4:6) If we have received Jesus as our Savior, we will have His light shining in our soul. Satan will have no power to destroy us. He may try to trip us up, but he cannot conquer us.

"Finally, my brethren, be strong in the Lord and in the power of His might. Put on the whole armor of God, that you may be able to stand against the wiles of the devil. For we do not wrestle against flesh and

blood, but against principalities, against powers, against the rulers of the darkness of this age, against spiritual hosts of wickedness in the

heavenly places. Therefore take up the whole armor of God, that you may be able to withstand in the evil day, and having done all, to stand." (Ephesians 6:10-13). We need to put on this armor daily. It is our protection against all the evil Satan wants to throw at us. Notice that this is a defensive position. We do not want to take Satan on ourselves. The battle belongs to the Lord.

"For You are my lamp, O Lord; The Lord shall enlighten my darkness." (2 Samuel 22:29) The Light of Jesus chases away the dark and makes our path clear to see.

"This is the message which we have heard from Him and declare to you, that God is light and in Him is no darkness at all." (1 John 1:5) Not only did God create light, but God IS light, with no shadow of turning. And all darkness will have to flee!

~~~~~~~

Living in the darkness leaves us at the mercy of the devil. We open the door for all kinds of evil to enter our hearts and minds. **"BUT GOD"** …. The two most powerful words you can utter. Because God is mightier than Satan and all his demons combined. Darkness and light cannot exist at the same time.

How do we find our way out of the darkness of sin, and into the light of Jesus? We call on His name, repent of our sins, and choose to follow Him. So, If you find yourself stumbling in the darkness, tripped up and entangled in sin, turn on the Light! The light of Jesus Christ. The author and finisher of our faith. Because at the name of Jesus, darkness has to flee. He will not share His throne with anyone!

REFLECTION TIME

Consider the differences between the darkness of sin, and the light of Jesus Christ. How does that minister to you?

_____
_____
_____
_____
_____
_____
_____

Was there a time when you found yourself in a dark situation and called out to the Lord? How did He reveal Himself as the Light?

_____
_____
_____
_____
_____
_____
_____

Write out a prayer, thanking Jesus for the gift of Light, and for a way to escape the darkness.

_____
_____
_____
_____
_____
_____
_____

Thank you, Lord Jesus, for the power of Your Light. Thank you that all we have to do is call out Your name and Satan has to flee. Help us to put on our full armor to protect us from the wiles of the devil. In Your Name, Amen!

~~ ADDITIONAL NOTES ~~

LIFE ON A CAT'S TERMS

(Having a Relationship with Jesus)

A few years ago, this white cat sauntered into my mom's house, just as if he lived there. We never saw him before, so we had no idea where he belonged. Mom instantly grew attached to him, and they bonded. He was unofficially adopted and given the name Elby. That's the initials L and B spelled out for the vets' records. Little Brat, Little Bug, Lover Boy, whatever suits the moment. When mom passed, he became the family cat.

Elby is a typical independent cat. He's aloof a lot of the time. You can walk through the door after a long day at work, and he barely stops his grooming routine to acknowledge your presence. It's as if to say, "Oh, it's you again….". He climbs on everything, making the bookcase, the desk, the back of the couch his domain for the moment. He thinks he owns the place. And let's be honest, they sort of do, don't they?

He has this one habit that drives me crazy. He loves to sharpen his already razor-sharp claws on the door jam, leaving scratches and peeled paint in his wake. He knows he is not supposed to do this, because he will stop when you reprimand him. One day, though, as he was clawing, I yelled at him to stop. I kid you not-he nonchalantly slid down the wall, giving me this bored look the entire time. The only thing missing was the yawn.

As I said, he's aloof. Until he needs something. He loves to cry out for attention at 4:00 in the morning. And heaven forbid his bowl is empty, or his litter box is not. He doesn't like to be picked up, but when he wants to be scratched, he will climb all over you. But don't even think about scratching below the shoulders or you are going to get a quick nip from him!

~~~~~~~

A good description of Elby's attitude is "leave me alone until I need you". Then I want you there for me. And on my terms. Sometimes we take that attitude in our relationship with the Lord. We love the whole salvation idea. We love the blessings that are bestowed upon us as His children. But we want to live this Christian life on our terms. Be there when I need you, Lord. But leave me alone in the meantime.

Sorry folks, but it doesn't work that way. God wants a relationship with us. That's what sets Christianity apart from religions. It requires a give and take attitude. He isn't a magic genie just waiting to fulfill our every desire. Far from it. We are to have an interactive relationship. There are several passages that are calls for action on our part for this healthy relationship.

A CALL TO ACTION

"Draw near to God, and He will draw near to you..." (James 4:8) We can't have an intimate relationship with Jesus if we hold Him back at arm's length.

"Rejoice always, pray without ceasing, in everything give thanks; for this is the will of God in Christ Jesus for you." (1 Thessalonians 5:16-18) If we apply these 3 commandments, we will have a fruitful walk with Him.

"Come to Me, all you who labor and are heavy laden, and I will give you rest." (Matthew 11:28) He beckons to us to come when life just gets too much. He promises to restore and renew us.

"Ask, and it will be given to you; seek, and you will find; knock, and it will be opened to you. For everyone who asks receives, and he who seeks finds, and to him who knocks it will be opened." (Matthew 7:7-8)

This applies when we are asking, seeking, knocking, all in His will. It's not a blanket promise that is applied when we are seeking our own desires.

GOD'S PROMISE

"And you will seek Me and find Me when you search for Me with all your heart." (Jeremiah 29:13) He promises to be there for us when we genuinely seek Him.

"If My people who are called by My name will humble themselves, and pray and seek My face, and turn from their wicked ways, then I will hear from heaven and will forgive their sin and heal their land. Now My eyes will be open and My ears attentive to prayer made in this place." (2 Chronicles 7:14-15) A promise originally made to the Jewish people, but if we want to see a change in our lives, then we need to come to Him in repentance.

As you can see, all these passages require action on our part. He is calling us into a relationship with Him. He is essentially saying, "this is what I want to give to you. But I want you to do your part as well". He wants to bestow blessings on us because He is good. But He won't indulge us simply to gain our love.

I need to make something clear here. All these scriptures are a call to action, but they are not required for salvation. That was already dealt with on the Cross. He paid the price ahead of time. We THEN need to do this, and only this:

"Repent therefore and be converted, that your sins may be blotted out, so that times of refreshing may come from the presence of the Lord." (Acts 3:19) There's that word again, "repent". We need to seek forgiveness for our sins which separate us from Jesus.

So, in wrapping up, Jesus is seeking a genuine relationship with us. He longs to hear from us. His Word is His love letter to us. Do we treat it as special as a letter from a loved one? Do we give of ourselves to Jesus, or do we look at Him as just someone from whom we get things? Are we obedient to His commands, or do we say, "Not so, Lord?" Some things to ponder, that's for sure.

REFLECTION TIME

Take a good, honest look at how you nurture your relationship with Jesus. Is He the Lord and love of your life? Or does He take a back seat most the time? Write your thoughts below.

_____

_____

_____

_____

_____

_____

_____

What are some areas that you need to commit to improving your relationship? Perhaps it is learning more of His Word, spending more time in prayer. Letting go of things that hinder your walk with Him. Write them out, commit to them, and decide on a plan of action.

_____

_____

_____

_____

_____

_____

_____

Write a prayer of thanksgiving for God's love and seek Him out to draw closer to Him.

_____

_____

_____

_____

_____

_____

_____

Thank You, Jesus, that You are a good, good Father who loves us and desires to be with us. We want to have a relationship with you. Help us to draw closer to You. Put a passion in our hearts for your Word. In Your name, Amen!

~~ ADDITIONAL NOTES ~~

~~ DAY 23 ~~

ON THE WINGS OF EAGLES

(God's Provision of Strength)

Here in the Pacific Northwest, bird watching is a favorite pastime. Every winter, we are treated to the annual migration of Snow geese and Trumpeter swans coming down from Siberia and Alaska. It is so fun to see the fields white with these birds, and when they get stirred up, their "honking" is almost deafening. I love watching them fly in groups overhead, their necks outstretched, honking away.

Another sight we look forward to every winter is the migration of eagles. They come to the area, returning each year to their nests (which are HUGE!) to bear their young. I have always found them to be such majestic birds. For some reason, I think of Walter Mondale when I see a picture of one full face!

The bald eagle was chosen June 20, 1782, as the emblem of the United States because of its long life, powerful strength and majestic looks, and also because it was then believed to exist only on this continent.

These birds have fascinating instincts. They are powerful, able to soar for hours due to the dynamics of their wings. Their grip is believed to be ten times stronger than a human hand's strength. They mate for life, choosing a new mate only when the first one dies.

~~~~~~~

The eagle, in the Bible, symbolizes power, strength, protection. These are things that we strive to achieve, but so often it is such a struggle. God

112

offers these to us freely. It comes with the privilege of being His children.

GOD'S PROMISE OF PROTECTION

"You have seen what I did to the Egyptians, and how I bore you on eagles' wings and brought you to Myself." (Exodus 19:14) God said this to Moses when he was leading the Israelites out of Egypt. God provided His protection. He bore them up on the strength of His wings.

"As an eagle stirs up its nest, hovers over its young, spreading out its wings, taking them up, carrying them on its wings, so the LORD alone led him, and there was no foreign god with him." (Deuteronomy 32:11-12) This passage speaks of protection, comparing how the eagle cares for its young, just as the Lord cares for and protects us.

GOD'S PROVISION FOR STRENGTH

"But those who wait on the Lord Shall renew their strength; they shall mount up with wings like eagles, they shall run and not be weary, they shall walk and not faint." (Isaiah 40: 31) This is probably the most familiar scripture in the Bible regarding eagles. The Lord will provide supernatural strength that the world cannot muster. The key here is waiting upon the Lord. It is far better to wait upon the Lord, do things in His power and might, then to get in there with my fumbling ways, just getting weary with the struggle. He makes things so much easier!

"And He said to me, 'My grace is sufficient for you, for My strength is made perfect in weakness.' Therefore most gladly I will rather boast in my infirmities, that the power of Christ may rest upon me." (2 Corinthians 12:9) God promises to care for us, to strengthen us when we are weak, and to lift us up when we are downtrodden. He will help us to soar on eagles' wings! We can then give God the glory, knowing that it wasn't because of our efforts that we were victorious.

"The Lord is my strength and song, and He has become my salvation; He is my God, and I will praise Him; My father's God, and I will exalt Him." (Exodus 15:2) Isn't it amazing that He is our strength, our salvation, and is worthy to be praised and exalted!

"The Lord is my strength and my shield; My heart trusted in Him, and I am helped; Therefore my heart greatly rejoices, and with my song I will praise Him." (Psalm 28:7) The psalmist recognized that it was God that gave him victory in the battle and is singing praises to his Lord.

~~~~~~~

People trying to do things in their strength reminds me of a story I heard a lifeguard share. One of the most challenging things they have to deal with when pulling someone to safety is the panic that sets in. The person fights and struggles, risking both of them drowning. Sometimes he wants to slug the person and knock him out, so he can pull him to safety! The best thing for you to do, he shared, was not to panic, but to relax and let him do his job.

Doesn't that also apply with our walk with Jesus? We fight and struggle against the situation, just getting weaker and more frustrated. Sinking into that quicksand. But if we let God be our strength, He will lift us up and give us the strength to get through the trial.

The next time you are weary and broken, feeling there is no more strength left in your body, take it to Jesus. Call out to Him to lift the heavy burden, raise you up on eagles wings, and give you the strength you need to carry on. Then praise Him for doing just that!

~~~~~~~

REFLECTION TIME

Ponder the scriptures above. How would you compare eagles to God's provision of strength?

_____

_____

_____

_____

_____

_____

Think about a time when you felt God's strength. How did it help you through your difficulty?

_____

_____

_____

_____

_____

_____

Write a prayer asking the Lord to provide you with His supernatural strength when you are feeling weak or helpless.

_____

_____

_____

_____

_____

_____

Thank you, Lord, for your promise to care for us and to strengthen us in our times of weakness. Help us to rely on Your strength, and not on our own devices. Help us to remember to seek you in our distress, and to turn all our cares upon You. In Your precious name, Amen!

PSSST...DID YOU HEAR?

(Gossip)

Gossip. Juicy, savory, irresistible. Not only does it feel good going in the ear, but it's just as satisfying coming out of the mouth. Some people have radar antennas for any dirt they can get on someone. They don't even have to know the person.

The more negative, the better. I could say to someone, "Susie is the nicest person I know." It might garner a small response. But if I said to that same person. "Susie is the meanest person ever!" Boy, the ears perk up. "Why?? What did she do??" Then the firestorm begins.

Here's another form of gossip. People can say things without really saying them. It's all in the tone and the implication of the words. For example, at work the other day, some mentioned that "John" was out with an injury. "That's what I have been told." Wink, wink. The facts of the story were presented as one way, but the voice inflection implied a whole different scenario. My curiosity was piqued, but given the person who shared this with me, I thought better not to respond. Rule of thumb? If you don't want your words repeated, then don't say them in the first place!

~~~~~~~

Gossip and backbiting may not appear to be as severe as something like murder. I heard a pastor say this once. When you spread gossip about somebody, you are essentially assassinating them in the other person's eyes. Go back to Susie. If you respond with, "well she's not as nice as you think she is. She has done this or that...". Suddenly I am filled with conflicting thoughts about her. Or I may pass judgment on her, not even knowing her! And once it is out there, it's hard to correct the information. That's why social media can be so dangerous. It spreads like wildfire. Have you noticed the newscasts always start with the bad stuff first? In 1982, rock singer Don Henley came out with a song called "Dirty Laundry". Boy did he hit the nail on the head with that one!

We Christians are often guilty of the sin of gossip as well. Only we dress it up differently. We add the phrase, "I am only telling you this, so you know how to pray…" Guess what? I don't need to know the juicy details. Because God already knows them. My job is to lift the situation up in prayer. Essentially this is what is happening when gossip hits the fan in the church. Not only are you damaging the character of the person, but you are causing strife and division among the congregation. And what if a visitor who is longing to know Jesus gets wind of this? It gives the church and the pastor a black eye. The damage is done.

WHAT ARE THE DANGERS BIBLICALLY?

"And even as they did not like to retain God in their knowledge, God gave them over to a debased mind, to do those things which are not fitting; being filled with all unrighteousness, sexual immorality, wickedness, covetousness, maliciousness; full of envy, murder, strife, deceit, evil-mindedness; they are **whisperers, backbiters,** *haters of God, violent, proud, boasters, inventors of evil things, disobedient to parents, undiscerning, untrustworthy, unloving, unforgiving, unmerciful; who, knowing the righteous judgment of God, that those who practice such things are deserving of death, not only do the same but also approve of those who practice them."* (Romans 1:28-31) Whoa! Did you catch that-whisperers and backbiters ranked up there with murder?? Oh, my! Remember the pastor's comment about character assassination…. And if we eagerly listen to the gossip, we are just as guilty as the talebearer.

"A perverse man sows strife, and a whisperer separates the best of friends." (Proverbs 16:28) Gossip does a lot of damage, often irreversible.

"A fool's mouth is his destruction, and his lips are the snare of his soul. The words of a talebearer are like tasty trifles, and they go down into the inmost body." (Proverbs 18:7-8) Unlike healthy food, they rot the gut.

"And the tongue is a fire, a world of iniquity. The tongue is so set among our members that it defiles the whole body and sets on fire the course of nature; it is set on fire by hell." (James 3:6) Pretty serious stuff, this gossip.

WHAT SHOULD BE OUR RESPONSE?

"A talebearer reveals secrets, but he who is of a faithful spirit conceals a matter." (Proverbs 11:13) In other words, keep your mouth shut!

"Whoever guards his mouth and tongue keeps his soul from troubles." (Proverbs 21:23) Kind words edify, harsh words tear down.

"I say then: Walk in the Spirit, and you shall not fulfill the lust of the flesh." (Galatians 5:16). Resist the urge to engage in gossip, either by spreading it or even listening to it. As Barney Fife, the deputy on *The Andy Griffith Show* always said, "Nip it! Nip it in the bud!" Douse the flame that is right in front of you.

Don't be the matchstick for the gossip flame. If you have an issue about something, instead of complaining to everyone around you, go to the person directly involved. Clear the air, get the facts straight. But make sure your motives are pure.

~~~~~~~

We're all guilty of wanting to indulge in a little gossip now and then. It is human nature. Be honest-don't you scan the tabloid headlines when you are in line at the grocery store? Talk about spreading lies and dirt! But the Bible is clear about the dangers of it. You can severely damage a person's reputation. The next time you get the urge to spill, ponder this passage:

"Finally, brethren, whatever things are true, whatever things are

noble, whatever things are just, whatever things are pure, whatever
things are lovely, whatever things are of good report, if there is any
virtue and if there is anything praiseworthy—meditate on these things.
The things which you learned and received and heard and saw in me,
these do, and the God of peace will be with you.". (Philippians 4:8-9).
Isn't that much more satisfying to the soul than carving out that pound of
flesh?

REFLECTION TIME

Think about a time when you engaged in some "friendly" gossip? How did it impact the way you thought about the person, or situation?

_____

_____

_____

_____

_____

_____

After studying the passages on gossip, how would you have handled that situation differently?

_____

_____

_____

_____

_____

Write out a prayer asking God to reveal to you how you can turn those temptations to gossip into opportunities of edification and how to diffuse the situation in a loving matter.

_____

_____

_____

_____

_____

_____

~~~~~~~

Dear Father: Thank you for the gift You have given us to verbally communicate with each other. But as Your word says, the tongue is like a flame of fire. Help us to use it for kindness, encouragement, and love rather than tearing others down for the sake of our own satisfaction. We want to have that peace with you that Your Word describes. In Your name, Amen!

~ DAY 25 ~

SPIRITUAL EARPLUGS

(Stubbornness)

The world is one noisy place. It seems impossible to have a quiet time; to be able to shut out all the noise and chaos of the world.

There are nights where I can fall asleep on the couch with every light on and the television blaring. Sometimes I can hardly keep my eyes open. Dragging myself up to go to bed is a monumental task. But strangely enough, when I get into bed, in order to sleep I need to have complete silence and total darkness. A light peeking through the curtain drives me nuts. So I have blackout curtains and industrial earplugs. The weird thing with earplugs, though, is if they are inserted really good, you can hear your pulse beating, and the air going in and out of your nose. That can be a bit distracting as well!

Some people use "virtual" earplugs when they don't want to hear what they need to as well. They stick their fingers in their ears, or cover them up and say, "Nah, nah, nah, I can't hear you!" Just like a child.

We can put spiritual earplugs in as well. There are a lot of hard sayings in the Bible. Things we don't want to read, hear, or apply to our lives. We pick and choose what we like about the Bible. Some churches cater to that. They don't address the sin issue, the end times, whatever may be uncomfortable. They don't want to offend anyone. The strategy is let's not tell people they are going to hell. We will tell them how to have a good life now. The bottom line is that they want people to keep coming back and fill their pews (and maybe their coffers?) That's so contrary to what God teaches.

THE FOLLY OF SPIRITUAL DEAFNESS

"For the time will come when they will not endure sound doctrine, but according to their own desires, because they have itching ears, they will heap up for themselves teachers; and they will turn their ears away from the truth and be turned aside to fables." (2 Timothy 4:3-4) People will only want to hear what makes them feel good. And there many churches more than happy to accommodate them. But they will be led astray.

"Son of man, you dwell in the midst of a rebellious house, which has eyes to see but does not see, and ears to hear but does not hear; for they are a rebellious house." (Ezekiel 12:2). Not being willing to hear what God has for us is a form of rebellion.

"But they refused to heed, shrugged their shoulders, and stopped their ears so that they could not hear." (Zechariah 7:11). Can't you just picture people doing that? Unfortunately, sticking your head in the sand, or your fingers in your ears, does not change the truth.

"But everyone who hears these sayings of Mine, and does not do them, will be like a foolish man who built his house on the sand." (Matthew 7:26) The Word is to build us up and strengthen us. Failing to listen to God gives us a weak foundation that will topple with the slightest force.

"He who is of God hears God's words; therefore you do not hear, because you are not of God." (John 8:47) When people are not a follower of Christ, the words of the Bible just don't make sense.

THE BENEFITS OF LISTENING

"Therefore let that abide in you which you heard from the beginning. If what you heard from the beginning abides in you, you also will abide in the Son and in the Father." (1 John 2:24) The positive side of listening to God! Abiding in Jesus is the best place to be.

"My sheep hear My voice, and I know them, and they follow Me." (John 10:27) If we don't hear and follow Jesus, then we are like lost

sheep, easy prey for the ravenous wolves. But if we know His voice, we will know which way to go.

"So then faith comes by hearing, and hearing by the word of God." (Romans 10:17) When we take in God's Word, our faith becomes stronger.

"But be doers of the Word, and not hearers only, deceiving yourselves. For if anyone is a hearer of the Word and not a doer, he is like a man observing his natural face in a mirror; for he observes himself, goes away, and immediately forgets what kind of man he was. But he who looks into the perfect law of liberty and continues in it, and is not a forgetful hearer but a doer of the work, this one will be blessed in what he does." (James 1:22-25) Not only are we instructed to be hearers of the Word, but we are to obey and apply it. There are blessings attached to the promise!

~~~~~~~

It can be tough to hear the hard sayings. Even tougher to obey them. But if we do, He promises to reward our obedience. One thing is for sure, though. We will be far better off to hear and follow the words of Jesus rather than the words of Satan. Seems like a no-brainer to me!

REFLECTION TIME

Has there been a time when you have put in your spiritual earplugs? What was the outcome?

_____

_____

_____

_____

_____

_____

What would you do differently in the same situation?

_____

_____

_____

_____

_____

_____

Write out a prayer asking Jesus to help you hear, understand, and apply the scriptures to your life.

_____

_____

_____

_____

_____

_____

Thank you heavenly Father, that you love us enough to teach us clearly the hard things. This Christian life can be challenging at times. Give us the ears to hear what the Spirit has to say and to willingly obey what You command. Help us to remember that Your way is always better than our finite ways. Thank you Jesus. Amen!

~~ DAY 26 ~~

THE DUSTY SWORD

(Studying Your Bible)

Many years ago, I worked in a Christian bookstore. We sold our share of Bibles. When someone would come in looking for one, there were questions we asked to help narrow it down to the perfect fit — questions like what translation, font size, type of binding, etc. It disturbed me when the first criterium was the cover. "I want a blue Bible with flowers, gold edges, and a pretty ribbon marker." Ok, but what about the inside? Now they have "coloring Bibles" that come with colored pencils so you can draw out your favorite scripture. Hmmm.... jury's still out on that one for me. I am a doodler. I doodle on EVERYTHING! Still, I think that's carrying it a bit too far. We are distracted enough when we read our Bibles. Now we are going to start coloring while studying?? I guess whatever floats your boat.

I read an alarming statistic recently. Biblical illiteracy is at an all-time low, which is perplexing because the Bible is the best-selling book of all time. When polled, people were hard-pressed to name even five of the ten commandments, some thought Billy Graham gave the sermon on the mount, and some even believed that Joan of Arc was Noah's wife! (That also shows historical illiteracy...). The frightening part is that so many self-proclaimed "born again Christians" are part of this crowd.

A greater travesty is what is coming out of our pulpits these days. So many churches are abandoning the Word of God for programs and flashy sanctuaries to draw the masses to their "feel good" churches. It's a lot harder these days to find a church that teaches FROM the Bible let alone through it. They want people to know all about God's favor and how to have it all here on earth. One former "Positive thinking" pastor stood in the pulpit and actually said the greatest sin is lack of self-esteem. I

125

believe, sir, it is blasphemy of the Holy Spirit. Oy, vey! It is very disturbing to me when I walk into a church and I don't see people carrying a Bible. Isn't that the textbook we are supposed to learn from?

Wherever you want to lay the blame for this, the bottom line is the responsibility lies at our doorstep. And it is a dangerous position to be in not to know the Word of God. It is the most potent weapon in our arsenal against the wiles of the devil. It is our instruction manual on how to navigate this life as Jesus commands us to.

Many times we buy these pretty Bibles, with the full intention of reading them every day. But so often it happens that the pretty Bible ends up on a shelf, just collecting dust. Now I ask you-how is that going to help you stay strong in your Christian walk?

~~~~~

THE POWER OF THE WORD

"For the word of God is living and powerful, and sharper than any two-edged sword, piercing even to the division of soul and spirit, and of joints and marrow, and is a discerner of the thoughts and intents of the heart." (Hebrews 4:12) It cuts to the very core of man.

"All Scripture is given by inspiration of God and is profitable for doctrine, for reproof, for correction, for instruction in righteousness, that the man of God may be complete, thoroughly equipped for every good work." (2 Timothy 3:16-17) There's that big little word-ALL. All means all, and all is what it means.

"Now out of His mouth goes a sharp sword, that with it He should strike the nations. And He Himself will rule them with a rod of iron." (Revelation 19:15) This passage refers to the second coming of Jesus, and simply with the Word of God, He will strike down evil. Now that's powerful!

HOW IT BENEFITS US

"How can a young man cleanse his way? By taking heed according to

Your word." (Psalm 119:9) Not only do we need to read the Word, but we need to obey it.

"Your word is a lamp to my feet and a light to my path." (Psalm 119:105) It will guide us in our daily travels through this life, keeping us on the right path.

"This Book of the Law shall not depart from your mouth, but you shall meditate in it day and night, that you may observe to do according to all that is written in it. For then you will make your way prosperous, and then you will have good success." (Joshua 1:8) We need to study the Word of God, get it into our hearts and minds, so that we can draw on it when we need it.

~~~~~~~~

When military fighters prepare for battle, they always keep their equipment clean and in good repair. They practice on the shooting range, so they are ready for the real thing. So it is with the Bible. We need to be using our weapon. But we don't use it to slay one another; rather, we use it to discern the truth from the lies, to know how to live a life that is pleasing to God, and to thwart the enemy when he attacks. Even Jesus used scripture to combat the devil. But if it lies dusty on a shelf somewhere, it will do us no good. So clean it off, open it up, and start reading it!

REFLECTION TIME

Have you fallen victim to the "I will read it later" syndrome? If so, what has kept you from spending quality time in God's Word?

_____
_____
_____
_____
_____
_____
_____

Think about a plan of how you can dig into the Word on a daily basis. Write it out here.

_____
_____
_____
_____
_____
_____
_____

Write out a prayer asking God to help you to commit to your new reading plan. Take a "get to" instead of a "got to" approach to learning of His Word.

_____
_____
_____
_____
_____
_____
_____

Thank you, Jesus, for the power of Your sword. It is such a privilege to be able to hear what You have to say about things. Thank you for this beautiful love letter. Help us to hide it in our hearts. In Your precious name, Amen!

～ ADDITIONAL NOTES ～

~~ DAY 27 ~~

THE GRASS IS GREENER ON THE OTHER SIDE

(God's Plan for Each of Us)

We spend a lot of time looking at what other people have and comparing it to our circumstances. It seems we are never satisfied. I went to visit a friend recently. She has a beautiful, thriving garden. There are all kinds of delicious looking veggies, some pretty flowers, and an excellent layout for her garden area. Then I came home to mine. Whaaahh!! Weeds, droopy leaves, leggy vines. It would never make the cover of a garden magazine, that's for sure! My excuse is that she must have a lot more time than I do. More likely she MAKES the time for her garden.

How often we envy what others have. From our vantage point, the grass is definitely greener on the other side. Sometimes, though, if you look closely, what you thought was a beautiful, healthy lawn has got some weeds growing in there. Last spring, everyone's yard looked like a big yellow field. In reality, they were giant patches of dandelion, which turned to seed and blew everywhere! I can only imagine what they will look like this year.

We don't always know what burdens another person may be carrying. Yes, they seem to be blessed way above what we have. But have you considered that those blessings may have come at a significant cost? Maybe that person has a zeal for living because she came very close to dying from cancer. Or your neighbor has a beautiful home, but you didn't know he grew up in a gang infested slum. How about the gal with the heart that seems to love everyone? The only "love" she found as a child was from the back of her daddy's hand.

130

Spiritually, it can work the same way. We seem to think this person is getting so many more blessings from God than we are. But we don't know the cross they are carrying. Nor is it any of our business why God is blessing them a certain way. I am reminded of a passage spoken by Jesus to Peter:

"Jesus said to him, 'If I will that he remain till I come, what is that to you? You follow Me.'" (John 21:22). Jesus had just laid out Peter's upcoming fate. Peter sees John walking by and asks, "what about him?" Essentially, Jesus is telling Pete to mind his own business.

Jesus has put a unique calling on each of our lives. Some are called to be in the public arena with a lot of notoriety. Others are called to work behind the scenes. Some are blessed with financial success, while still others are always paycheck to paycheck.

~~~~~~

Getting back to my friend. Not only does she have a beautiful garden, but she has a warm, loving home, a wonderful family, and a deep relationship with the Lord. They have much for which to be thankful. But there have been many, many trials to test their faith. They have been brought to the mat, so to speak. Because of their strong commitment to the Lord and to each other, they have weathered the storms and come through even stronger.

WE ARE TO RUN OUR OWN RACE

"But none of these things move me; nor do I count my life dear to myself, so that I may finish my race with joy and the ministry which I received from the Lord Jesus, to testify to the gospel of the grace of God." (Acts 20:24) Notice he said HIS race, the ministry that HE received. We are each to run our own race. Not our neighbor's, not our coworker's, but our own. Paul was called to a powerful ministry. He paid a heavy price along the way, though. In 2 Corinthians Ch 11, Paul listed

all the sufferings he experienced in his ministry (vs. 23-28). Yet through it all, he only boasted about Jesus Christ.

"Do you not know that those who run in a race all run, but one receives the prize? Run in such a way that you may obtain it." (1 Corinthians 9:24). God has a crown waiting just for you!

THE ENTRY FEE

"Then He said to them all, "If anyone desires to come after Me, let him deny himself, and take up his cross daily, and follow Me." (Luke 9:23) Let go of selfish ambitions, possessions that possess us, and relationships that get in the way of Jesus.

"And whoever does not bear his cross and come after Me cannot be My disciple." (Luke 14:27). Notice that we are called to bear our own cross. We are not accountable for anyone else's calling.

"For everyone to whom much is given, from him much will be required; and to whom much has been committed, of him they will ask the more." (Luke 12:48). A life following Jesus Christ can be a challenging one. We are expected to use what we are given all to the glory of God whether it be in a stadium in front of 50,000 people, or in a classroom of toddlers.

~~~~~~~~

How does this all tie together? Each one of us is on our own personal journey with the Lord. Our particular callings are designed by the Lord to accomplish His purpose. For some, the path is smooth; for others it is a road filled with hardship. Whichever one it is, we need to embrace the journey and walk the path with joy.

So, the next time you start peeking over the fence and coveting your neighbor's beautiful green lawn, don't concern yourself with what they appear to have. Just start watering your own patch of grass instead!

REFLECTION TIME

Have there been times when you have felt your life has fallen short compared to others? Think of one specific area and write it down here.

_____

_____

_____

_____

_____

_____

_____

Paul exhorts us to run our own race. What is God calling you to do that is uniquely yours?

_____

_____

_____

_____

_____

_____

Write a prayer asking God to help you keep your eyes focused on His calling on your life.

_____

_____

_____

_____

_____

_____

_____

Dear Jesus: Thank you that you have called each and every one of us to a race that is our own. Help us to "stay in our lane" and not be concerned with our fellow runners. Help us to find the joy in the journey along the way. Thank you that there is a prize waiting for us when we have finished that race and we see you face to face! What a glorious day that will be! In Your strong name, Amen!

~~ ADDITIONAL NOTES ~~

THE STATIN LADY

(The Cost of Following Jesus)

I was in the store the other day when a woman walked by me. She randomly asked me a question. "Is there a way to control cholesterol without taking meds?" Why she asked me this I don't know. Maybe I looked like I would know something about high cholesterol! I pondered the question then said, "Well, if you eat a healthy diet and exercise, you might be able to control it." She considered my answer, then responded, "Hmmm. I would rather eat the bacon and take the statin." Then she went on her way. Strange....

A lot of people approach life that way. They want to have all the benefits of something, but are not willing to put in the necessary work or make the needed changes to achieve those benefits. For example, you may want to have a strong, healthy body, but you don't want to put the work in at the gym or give up the fast food and sodas. Or I want to have a beautiful garden, but I don't want to put in the physical work required to make it beautiful. Our statin lady wanted to have the health benefits of the medication, but she didn't want to make the changes in her lifestyle, which no doubt contributed to the need for the meds in the first place!

~~~~~~~

Our relationship with Jesus can be approached the same way. Take Stanley, for instance. He was living a very worldly life. But finding it to be empty, he decided to give his life to Jesus. Stanley said the sinner's prayer, took the free Bible and went home. He was enthusiastic for a few days. Then he went to church the next Sunday. He heard a message about sin, how we are to turn away from it as followers of Christ. Uh-oh. You mean I have to give up what I enjoy? The partying, the booze, the potty mouth?? Can't I have my cake and eat it too? (Don't ask me to explain that expression!) Sacrifice??? I didn't sign up for that. I'm outta here!

A sad scenario, but it happens far too often. People get caught up in the moment of the crusade or the altar call. Their intentions are sincere. But here's an expression for you. *"The road to hell is paved with good intentions."*

WHAT IS THE COST?

"If anyone comes to Me and does not hate his father and mother, wife and children, brothers and sisters, yes, and his own life also, he cannot be My disciple. And whoever does not bear his cross and come after Me cannot be My disciple. For which of you, intending to build a tower, does not sit down first and count the cost, whether he has enough to finish it—" (Luke 14:26-27) Before we casually decide to follow Jesus we must first understand what He is asking of us. We must count the cost. But He does not mean to literally hate your family. But we must love Jesus more than we love anyone or anything else. We must also be willing to walk away from something if Jesus asks it of us.

"'If you want to be perfect, go, sell what you have and give to the poor, and you will have treasure in heaven; and come, follow Me.' But when the young man heard that saying, he went away sorrowful, for he had great possessions." (Matthew 19:21-22) This was the response Jesus gave to the rich young ruler, who had, on the surface, led a Godly life. Doing all that he could to earn his way to heaven. But when it came to giving up that one thing that Jesus felt was holding him back, his riches, he couldn't make the sacrifice. So he chose to walk away — the most tragic thing we can do. Jesus wasn't saying that his money would keep him out of heaven. But He knew this was a sticking point for the man. He was leading a selfish life, not a selfless life.

"Then He said to them all, 'If anyone desires to come after Me, let him deny himself, and take up his cross daily, and follow Me. For whoever desires to save his life will lose it, but whoever loses his life for My sake will save it. For what profit is it to a man if he gains the whole world, and is himself destroyed or lost?'" (Luke 9:23-25) Notice Jesus said to

them ALL. Not just a select few of us. But to everyone who wants to be His follower, and following means precisely that. We are to be wholly surrendered to Him.

~~~~~~~

We are asked to make sacrifices in our walk with Jesus. Not for salvation, that was already taken care of on the cross. But if we are going to claim the title of "Christian", which means follower of Christ, then we have to live a life that He is calling us to. We cannot sit here and say He is the Lord of our life, then when He calls us to something, we turn around and say, "No, Lord." If the answer is "no", then we have to ask ourselves, is He Lord or not?

What does it mean to deny myself? To be willing to renounce and relinquish my so-called right to plan or choose, and to recognize His lordship in all areas of my life. Not an easy task, to be sure. But the rewards are far greater than staying stuck in my own self-serving plan. Jesus said I have to lose my life to save it. Huh? I lose the self-centered, worldly focus to gain the riches of a Christ-centered life. Yes, it is unpopular, and it will often be a challenging road. But it will all be worth it. I promise. Better yet, Jesus promises it!

REFLECTION TIME

Is there something in your life that is holding you back in your walk with Jesus? Is it a relationship, a bad habit, an unhealthy attitude?

_____

_____

_____

_____

_____

_____

What do you need to do to overcome that stumbling block?

_____

_____

_____

_____

_____

_____

Write out a prayer asking God to reveal to you what you need to surrender and ask for the strength to accomplish this.

_____

_____

_____

_____

_____

_____

_____

Thank you, Lord Jesus, for paying the ultimate price for us, Your very life. Please reveal to us what we can give in return. Thank you that You will provide us with the tools that we need to make the sacrifice You are asking. We know that no matter what it is, it will pale in comparison to the sacrifice You made for us. We are so grateful that You love us lowly creatures that much. In Your name, Amen!

WEED AND FEED

(A Healthy, Spiritual "Garden")

Planting a garden can be very rewarding. From planning out your future harvest to setting up, weeding and watering, and then to finally enjoying the fruits of your labor as you reap the bountiful harvest.

I discovered this past summer that there is a lot more physical work to a garden than meets the eye. Yes, I was prepared for the digging of the soil, and the constant nurturing of the seedlings as they matured into productive plants. Oh, but the weeds!

Here is a phenomenon that I have never been able to grasp. Weeds grow EVERYWHERE! Wet ground, dry ground, cracks in the asphalt (now that one blows my mind!). And guess what? You can't water your garden without hitting the weeds too. Those nasty buggers horn in on every nutrient you have applied to your plants. They invade the space, seemingly overnight. Heaven forbid you let your guard down for a day or two. If you do, the next thing you know they are choking out your tender plants, just like an invading army. So, the ongoing battle of the backyard gardener is this: how to feed the good guys and keep the bad guys at bay.

~~~~~~~

My mind is much like that garden plot in the backyard; a garden that needs constant care, proper input, and fighting the never-ending battle of the enemy penetrating my thoughts. Whichever one I feed the most is what will determine the daily harvest: bountiful fruit or nasty old weeds.

So how do we go about creating and nurturing this mental garden that is pleasing to God?

STEP 1: PREPARE THE SOIL

"Blessed is the man who walks not in the counsel of the ungodly, nor stands in the path of sinners, nor sits in the seat of the scornful. But his delight is in the law of the Lord, and in His law, he meditates day and night. He shall be like a tree planted by the rivers of water, that brings forth its fruit in its season, whose leaf also shall not wither; and whatever he does shall prosper." (Psalm 1:1-3) It is vital to the health of our spiritual walk that we have our minds filled with the law (God's Word). If we are studying and meditating regularly, His Word will penetrate our hearts, guiding us in our walk with Jesus. We must saturate our minds with the healthy nutrients supplied by the Living Bread.

STEP 2: BE IN GOD'S WORD DAILY

"But He answered and said, 'It is written, 'Man shall not live by bread alone, but by every word of God.'" (Luke 4:4) It's essential to have that daily serving of God's Word so that when a sinful thought enters our mind (a temptation), we will be able to recognize it for what it is and know what course to take.

STEP 3: TAKE EVERY THOUGHT CAPTIVE

"For the weapons of our warfare are not carnal but mighty in God for pulling down strongholds, casting down arguments and every high thing that exalts itself against the knowledge of God, bringing every thought into captivity to the obedience of Christ, and being ready to punish all disobedience when your obedience is fulfilled." (2 Corinthians 10:4-6) Don't let evil thoughts take root. Let's face it. We are all human; subject to impure or unkind thoughts. Our mind is a battlefield. We are constantly wrestling between right and wrong. The enemy is relentlessly trying to bring us down. The important thing, like the weeds, is that we nip them in the bud!

"The Lord will guide you continually, and satisfy your soul in drought, and strengthen your bones. You shall be like a watered garden, and like a spring of water, whose waters do not fail." (Isaiah 58:11) Without water, our gardens will not grow. Without the Living Water, our souls will wither.

"Create in me a clean heart, O God, and renew a steadfast spirit within me." (Psalm 51:10) Think of a clean heart as pure, nutrient-rich soil that will produce strong, healthy thoughts and deeds.

STEP 4: FILL YOUR "GARDEN" WITH THE GOODNESS OF GOD

"Finally, brethren, whatever things are true, whatever things are noble, whatever things are just, whatever things are pure, whatever things are lovely, whatever things are of good report, if there is any virtue and if there is anything praiseworthy—meditate on these things. The things which you learned and received and heard and saw in me, these do, and the God of peace will be with you." (Philippians 4:8-10). These positive thoughts and attitudes are the result of the clean heart mentioned in Step 3. Peace will be our blessing.

"You will keep him in perfect peace, whose mind is stayed on You because he trusts in You." (Isaiah 26:3). Peace comes from a constant connection with the Master Peacemaker.

~~~~~~~

All these passages have a two-fold purpose. If we apply them to our daily walk with the Lord, we will be weeding and feeding at the same time. If we fill our minds with the goodness of the Lord, we will have a beautiful garden. If we use the wrong fertilizer and let the weeds (evil thoughts or habits) take root, then we will reap thorny bushes.

"For he who sows to his flesh will of the flesh reap corruption, but he who sows to the Spirit will of the Spirit reap everlasting life." (Galatians 6:8)

REFLECTION TIME

Committing to a daily schedule of reading God's Word is crucial in guarding our hearts and minds from the weeds of sin. Develop a plan that you can reasonably commit to, and write it below:

_____
_____
_____
_____
_____
_____
_____

The Scriptures tell us to take every thought captive. What does that look like to you? (Hint: read Philippians 4:8-10 above.)

_____
_____
_____
_____
_____
_____
_____

Write a prayer asking the Holy Spirit to reveal to you the strongholds in your heart and mind, to give you the strength to resist them, and to help you feed your mind with pure thoughts that are pleasing to God.

_____
_____
_____
_____
_____
_____
_____

Dear Lord Jesus: Thank You for Your Word. Thank You that You have given us the tools to develop a strong spiritual mindset. The scriptures empower us to resist the enemy, to tear down the strongholds and to clear out the weeds of sin. Help us to commit to feeding on Your Word every single day. In Your Strong Name, Amen!

~~ ADDITIONAL NOTES~~

~ DAY 30 ~

YOU WANT ME TO DO WHAT???

(Obedience)

Have you ever had a time when you felt God was telling you to do something, and you simply didn't want to do it? I had that experience recently. I was walking through the store at work when I passed an older woman. She was wearing a bright pink shirt that said she stood for this particular organization that I personally believe is very destructive. When I saw her shirt, steam came out of my ears! I muttered a comment under my breath as I passed her to express my displeasure. I was livid. Suddenly, I felt God say to pray for her. Ok! But it was a prayer along the lines of "Break her teeth, Lord!" Very loving, right? Then the scripture came to mind when Jesus was hanging on the cross and prayed ***"Father, forgive them for they know not what they do."*** (Luke 23:34) My obstinance caused me to respond, "she knows exactly what they do!" My heart was not in a compassionate or forgiving place. While I was wrestling with this, she kept popping up in my line of vision. I couldn't escape her! Then I started thinking about all of the heartache, suffering, and loss due to this organization, and my heart became broken. Just as God's is, I am sure. Tears filled my eyes. Just at that point, I heard a voice behind me say, "Excuse me." It was the pink shirt lady! "Do you know where the vinegar is?" she asked sweetly. I looked at her shirt, then at her face, and almost said no, just to be stubborn, but then I politely answered her question. "OK, God," I sighed. "I know you want me to pray for this woman's eyes to be opened. I get it."

144

Sometimes it feels as if God asks us to do the impossible. To pray for something or to love somebody when we feel that everything about it is wrong. But we need to remember that God died for every single person who ever walked the face of this earth. We are commanded to love others. We are not asked to be judge and jury, and withold love based on our verdict. Check these out:

THE LORD REQUIRES US TO LOVE

"A new commandment I give to you, that you love one another; as I have loved you, that you also love one another." (John 13:34) That is so hard sometimes, given we can be such an unlovable bunch!

"Therefore you shall love the Lord your God, and keep His charge, His statutes, His judgments, and His commandments always." (Deuteronomy 11:1) The only way we can be obedient in these matters is to have the Holy Spirit residing inside of us giving us the love that Jesus demonstrated.

I know my flesh soooo wants to do things my way. Stubborn as the day is long, sometimes! But God has a bigger and better plan in mind. If I am going to call myself a follower of Christ, that's what I need to be. The lady in the store didn't need my condemning attitude. She needed my prayers, just as the Lord was calling me to do.

THE ACT OF OBEDIENCE

"And being found in appearance as a man, He humbled Himself and became obedient to the point of death, even the death of the cross." (Philippians 2:8) Jesus demonstrated the ultimate act of obedience. It makes my stubbornness petty in comparison.

"But why do you call Me 'Lord, Lord,' and not do the things which I say?" (Luke 6:46). How often do we wrestle with that? These two words do not belong in the same sentence: "No" and "Lord". He cannot be Lord of our lives if we are going to defy Him.

Peter rebuked the Lord more than once. On one occasion, this was the response from Jesus: *"He rebuked Peter, saying, 'Get behind Me,*

Satan! For you are not mindful of the things of God, but the things of men.'" (Mark 8:33) Ouch! How would you like to hear that from Jesus!

OBEDIENCE BEYOND MEASURE

The old testament has several men who were asked to be obedient when it didn't make sense. In Genesis 22, Abraham was tested by God. He was asked to sacrifice his only son. Abraham was obedient almost to the point of the death of his son, but God intervened. Abe didn't know why God was asking him this, or what He was going to do, but he trusted and obeyed.

Noah was asked to build an ark and fill it with animals because God was going to flood the earth. (Genesis Ch. 6-7) Scholars estimate it took him 100-120 years to build it. Now, that's a lot of faith that God was going to keep His Word!

These two men, Abraham and Noah, were asked to do incredible things. And because of their obedience, God used them in mighty ways. Through Abraham came the blessings of all nations. Through Noah, a new earth was started after God brought judgment on the earth by flood.

~~~~~~~

Now we may not have such a dramatic calling on our lives, but obedience in everything no matter how big or small it may seem is required. But we shouldn't rely on blind faith. Like Abraham, our faith should be so secure in the Lord, that we don't question. We trust, and we believe. And we indeed do not utter the words, "No, Lord", as Peter did. It always resulted in a verbal spanking!

I am grateful for the blessings that the Lord gives us. Being disobedient not only disappoints the Lord but at the very least it robs us of those blessings and may very well prevent us from being used mightily.

So, if you wake up one day and hear God is telling you to build an ark, you might want to consider making a trip to the hardware store! Don't worry about what others think. The people probably thought Noah was a little "tetched" himself!

REFLECTION TIME

Think about a time when you were disobedient to God. How did you wrestle with it, and what was the outcome?

_____

_____

_____

_____

_____

_____

Read the account of Abraham in Genesis 22. How does his faith in the Lord encourage you?

_____

_____

_____

_____

_____

_____

Write out a prayer asking God for forgiveness for any obedience you have demonstrated, and to give you the strength and faith to follow His calling, especially when it doesn't make sense.

_____

_____

_____

_____

_____

_____

Dear Heavenly Father, we are a stiff-necked people. Prone to stubbornness and disobedience, always wanting to do things our way. Please forgive us for that and help us to trust and rest in You and your faithfulness. Help us to submit to you, our Lord and King! In Jesus Name, Amen!

FINISH YOUR RACE

(Finishing Strong)

Have you ever competed in a race-either a 5K, 10K, or even a marathon? It takes a lot of preparation, commitment and training to do well.

A few years ago, I got on a walking/jogging kick. I would walk to warm up, then jog for a minute, then walk for a minute. I alternated this pattern, slowly trying to increase the jogging time. I marked out a trail that equaled 5K, or 3.1 miles. I think I managed to get my time in the low 40 minute range.

So I decided to enter a 5K walk/run for charity. I wanted to support our Marine veterans. My motivation to get through the run was, if they can risk life and limb for me, I can surely walk for them! Now it's essential to train ahead of time, so by race day, your body is conditioned for the task at hand. And you can avoid the agony of de-feet! (Tee hee!) I finished mid-pack, which was good enough for me. I entered another one to walk for Alzheimer's. I walked in my mom's name, who had passed two weeks prior. That one turned into being more of a walk, as the serious runners were off somewhere else. I think I entered one or two more before I hung up my sneakers.

~~~~~~

This Christian life can be compared to a marathon run. The Apostle Paul used many athletic metaphors to describe our journey.

THE CHRISTIAN MARATHON

"Do you not know that those who run in a race all run, but one receives the prize? Run in such a way that you may obtain it. And everyone who competes for the prize is temperate in all things. Now they do it to obtain a perishable crown, but we for an imperishable crown. Therefore I run thus: not with uncertainty. Thus I fight; not as one who beats the air. But I discipline my body and bring it into subjection, lest, when I have preached to others, I myself should become disqualified." (1 Corinthians 9:24-27) Paul is comparing the discipline needed to win an athletic crown to each of us winning our own race to obtain our heavenly crown. It takes discipline in studying the Word, applying it, and being obedient to God.

"And also if anyone competes in athletics, he is not crowned unless he competes according to the rules." (2 Timothy 2:5) That adage applies: cheaters never win, and winners never cheat!

"Not that I have already attained or am already perfected; but I press on, that I may lay hold of that for which Christ Jesus has also laid hold of me. Brethren, I do not count myself to have apprehended; but one thing I do, forgetting those things which are behind and reaching forward to those things which are ahead, I press toward the goal for the prize of the upward call of God in Christ Jesus." (Philippians 3:12-14) For the disciplined Christian, the prize is not earthly rewards, but what Jesus has for us. We need to forget about the past, good or bad, and focus on our goal ahead. We should never rest on our laurels, being content with what God has done in our lives in the past. We need to keep seeking that higher calling.

PRESSING ON

*"Therefore we also, since we are surrounded by so great a cloud of witnesses, let us lay aside every weight, and the sin which so easily ensnares us, and let us run with endurance the race that is set before us, looking unto Jesus, the author and finisher of our faith, who for the joy that was set before Him endured the cross, despising the shame, and has sat down at the right hand of the throne of God." (*Hebrews

12:1-2) Jesus should be the prize for which we are striving. The joy, despite the suffering, was the accomplishment of His race, the cross. He finished it, and we are indeed the benefactors of the prize.

This particular verse reminds me of the day my mom entered into the joy of her Lord. She passed into heaven at about 3:20 a.m. Later that morning, as life has to go on, I was putting the trash cans out at the curb. As I was walking back up to the house, I suddenly got this picture in my mind of my mom standing in a group of about five other women. Her sister Maxine was one of them. They were all wearing simple white choir type robes. The ladies were hugging her and cheering for her. It made me feel good because at that moment I knew my mom had finished her race and was greeted by those who had gone before her. It was a beautiful picture, and it gave me peace and joy.

CROSSING THE FINISH LINE

Paul's final reference to a race came as he was near the end of his life. He shared these words with Timothy, his protégé. *"For I am already being poured out as a drink offering, and the time of my departure is at hand. I have fought the good fight, I have finished the race, I have kept the faith. Finally, there is laid up for me the crown of righteousness, which the Lord, the righteous Judge, will give to me on that day, and not to me only but also to all who have loved His appearing."* (2 Timothy 4:6-8). What beautiful words, and something that we all as Christians should strive for!

~~~~~~~

I eventually gave up my 5K career. The knees barked too much, and frankly, I just got tired of it. But I never want to give up on my Christian walk marathon. Sure there are hills and valleys, not always smooth paths. Potholes and barricades sometimes pop up out of nowhere. I may even feel at times that the road ahead of me has been washed out. I may be just too pooped to go on. But we have that wonderful encouragement from the Lord, *"Come to Me, all you who labor and are heavy laden, and I will give you rest. Take My yoke upon you and learn from Me, for I am gentle and lowly in heart, and you will find rest for your souls. For My yoke is easy and My burden is light."* (Matthew 11:28-30)

Sometimes we just need to breathe, and let Him restore us. Then throw on our Spiritual sneakers and get right back in the race.

What a life! What a Savior!

REFLECTION TIME

How would you describe your personal race? Are you sprinting then pooping out, or are you focused on the long haul?

_____

_____

_____

_____

_____

_____

_____

What spiritual "muscles" do you need to strengthen in your race? Is it prayer time, servanthood, sharing your faith, digging deeper into the Word perhaps?

_____

_____

_____

_____

_____

_____

_____

Write a prayer asking Jesus how you may draw closer to Him and how to finish your race strong.

_____

_____

_____

_____

_____

_____

Dear Heavenly Father: Thank you for those beautiful words of encouragement from your servant Paul. Thank you for his example of how to be victorious in our Christian walk. Give us the strength to keep pressing on, and to keep our eye on the prize. What a glorious day that will be when we see You face to face. In Your precious name, Amen!

~~ ADDITIONAL NOTES ~~

CONCLUSION

Now that you have made your way through the devotionals, I pray that you have enjoyed your travels. Hopefully you have seen yourself in some of the scenarios that were presented. But even more importantly, I pray that, through the studying of the scriptures, you have gained a deeper love for God's Word, and a better understanding of how He is part of each and every moment of our crazy lives. And remember,

It's all about Jesus!

Please check out my website

www.itsallaboutjesusthelivingword.com

for free resources, updates on upcoming projects, and a prayer closet where you can leave prayer requests.

Thanks for hanging out with me every day—

I'll catch you in volume 2!

May God bless you, and keep you, may He make His face to shine upon you, and give you peace!

ACKNOWLEDGMENTS

Very few books come to see the light of day without a host of participants. So I would like to take a moment to acknowledge and extend my heartfelt thanks to the following "partners":

First and foremost, I am eternally thankful to Jesus Christ, the Author and Finisher of my faith, and the core topic of these devotionals. I can't wait to see You face to face! To You be all the glory.

To my earthly partners in crime:

Pamela: Your editing kept me grounded, and smoothed out the rough patches. (Not to mention curbing my tendency for sarcastic humor!) I appreciate your prayers and encouragement more than I can say. Can't wait to partner with you on the next project!

To my "roomies": Pat, my sister, both earthly and in Christ. Thanks for letting me bounce ideas off you, for putting up with my stuff all over the place, your faithful prayers, and for allowing me to do what I needed to do. I can't count how many hours you saw my head buried in the computer! Levi, who became the subject of the first installment I wrote when the book was still a blog thought. Missing you terribly, little bug! And Elby, also a topic, who liked to contribute by walking all over my keyboard and totally changing my thoughts. You little rascal!

Kaylin: Thanks for being my "beta" reader and cheerleader. There were many days of frustration and confusion. Your enthusiasm and encouragement was a great motivator.

Pastor Brian: You unwittingly gave me a number of these topics through your solid Biblical teaching. Thank you for staying the course. It was amazing how many times you used the very same scripture reference I had been working with the previous day. Confirmation, I would say!

The entire SPS team: Chandler, Sean, and my coach Gary-your professional guidance made a huge difference in how this book turned out. And to the entire mastermind community, a group of fellow aspiring writers. Although we have different stories to tell, we all share the same dream-to get those stories out of our heads and onto paper. A fabulously encouraging group of men and women.

Finally: to the host of faithful servants, who were unknowingly used by God to encourage me to write. Some of you planted seeds many years ago, others came along with your watering cans. A couple of you sprayed me full-on with a hose! I hate to say it, but sometimes it takes a virtual 2-by-4 alongside the head to get my attention! Message received... (thanks for the lumps!)

ABOUT THE AUTHOR

Deborah Bedson is a native of California. Desiring a more rural lifestyle, she moved to North Washington State in 2015, where she fell in love with the beauty of God's creation. Time spent working in the Christian retail industry gave her a love for spreading the Word of God. After many encouraging words from family and friends to write (and much prayer about how to do this), "It's All About Jesus-the Living Word" was born. It is her prayer that the reader will develop a deeper, more meaningful connection to God.

For related resources, check these out:

Website: www.itsallaboutjesusthelivingword.com

email: itsallaboutjesusthelivingword@gmail.com

Please join our Facebook group:

ITS ALL ABOUT JESUS THE LIVING WORD

THANK YOU

FOR READING MY BOOK!

I really appreciate all of your feedback,
and I love hearing what you have to say.

I need your input to make the next version
of this book and my future books better.

Please leave me an honest review on Amazon
letting me know what you thought of the book.

Thanks so much!

Deborah Bedson

Made in the USA
Monee, IL
24 September 2019